WILLIAM BARRETT

TRAVIS

William Barret Travis
Painting by H. A. McArdle
— Courtesy Texas State Archives

WILLIAM BARRETT
TRAVIS
A Biography

Archie P. McDonald

EAKIN PRESS ★ Austin, Texas

Revised Edition, 1995

Published in the United States of America
By Eakin Press
A Division of Sunbelt Media, Inc.
P.O. Drawer 90159 ★ Austin, TX 78709-0159

ISBN 0-89015-656-5

this book is dedicated to
JUDY
because of her feel for life, for people, and her
intuitive understanding of mountains and streams

Casey Biggs as Travis in the IMAX film Alamo . . . the Price of Freedom. *Biggs portrays Travis as a sensitive, yet determined young commander in what is probably the most viewed, longest running and largest Alamo film to date, showing at the San Antonio IMAX Theatre on a six-story screen.* — Courtesy Rivertheatre Associates, Ltd.

Contents

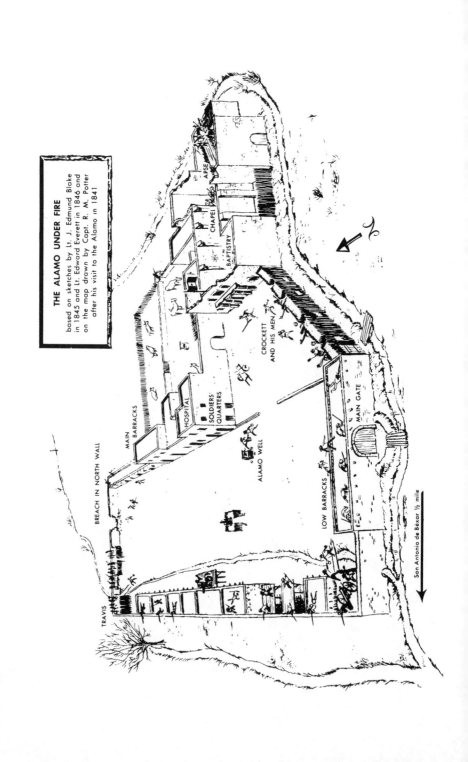

THE ALAMO UNDER FIRE

based on sketches by Lt. J. Edmund Blake in 1845 and Lt. Edward Everett in 1846 and on the map drawn by Capt. R. M. Potter after his visit to the Alamo in 1841

APSE

CHAPEL

BAPTISTRY

CROCKETT AND HIS MEN

MAIN BARRACKS

HOSPITAL

SOLDIERS' QUARTERS

ALAMO WELL

MAIN GATE

LOW BARRACKS

BREACH IN NORTH WALL

TRAVIS

San Antonio de Béxar ½ mile

Acknowledgment

IT HARDLY requires admission that any publication such as this places one in the debt of a great many people. Simple "thank yous" are never enough; it may only be hoped that some small part of what is being communicated is understood. I would like to thank especially the following individuals and institutions for their assistance in the research, writing, and publication of this biography.

First, I want to thank Ruby Mixon of Fort Worth for doing so much of the ground breaking in the study of Travis. Ms. Mixon kindly permitted the examination of her work, making so much of mine that much easier. George Singleton of Monroeville, Alabama also deserves a special word of thanks. He conducted my wife and me over Monroe County; to Old Claiborne, to an isolated and nearly forgotten Jewish cemetery, to a steaming-hot courthouse attic, and—when my car broke down—to a competent mechanic. Other Alabamians who helped include Mrs. W. E. Deer of Claiborne, Alabama, where Travis practiced law. Mrs. Deer lives in the century and a half old James Dellet home, which contains many of his papers which were helpful in studying Travis' Alabama years. Raymond Fountain, also of Monroeville, met us in a road side cafe to spin stories of local Travis tradition. At Montgomery,

State Archivist Milo Howard and a venerable Alabama record keeper, William Letford, graciously made available their facilities. In Saluda, South Carolina, Motte J. Yarborough got up from a nap to rescue us from a "Wednesday afternoon," a traditional dead-time in rural South Carolina, to wander the backroads of Travis' youth. These are cherished new friends.

Support also came from older friends, mostly closer to home. Mr. Cooper Ragan of Houston, as usual, graciously opened his magnificent library of Texana; Ms. Pearl Travis of Chireno, one of the few Travis family members in Texas, gave permission to use her Travis family crest; Mrs. Wilma W. Riley of Houston sent genealogical information; David G. McComb now of Colorado State University helped with leg work in Austin; Frank Wardlaw and John H. Jenkins, distinguished Texas publishers, unknowingly gave tremendous encouragement when it was most needed; Ms. Ouida Dean shared her considerable language skills; and all I can say for Haskell Monroe of Texas A&M University is that old friends are the best.

John M. Kinney and Millicent Huff of the Texas State Library, the latter for helping with copies of Travis portraits, are appreciated; Robert Dalahite of the Rosenburg Library, Galveston, had the materials all waiting for me when I visited that island city; Ms. Madeleine Perez made our visit to the Daughters of the Republic of Texas Library at the Alamo profitable and enjoyable, and Mrs. Carolyn Ericson of Nacogdoches also aided in the use of the D.R.T. Museum at Austin; Chester Kielman allowed the use of the materials at the Department of Archives, University of Texas; and the staff at the San Jacinto Monument and at the Chambers and Liberty County courthouses and the Anahuac city library were most helpful. The many members of the staff of the Stephen F. Austin State University Library deserve, at least, appreciation and special commendation.

The Faculty Research Grant program, and the Faculty Development Program of Stephen F. Austin State Univer-

sity gave me encouragement and time to do some of the
work on this study. I wish to thank Dr. Ralph Steen,
SFASU President, and Dr. Robert S. Maxwell, Chairman
of the Department of History, for their understanding and
support; Dr. Richard Voigtel for his assistance in obtaining a Kempner Foundation Grant for a research trip; and
the National Endowment for the Humanities for its Young
Humanist Grant. Special thanks go to Dr. John T. Lewis,
III, Vice-President for Academic Affairs at Stephen F.
Austin State University, for securing a Tennaco Grant and
for his support.

Finally, I wish to thank two young Texans, Tucker Barrett and Christopher Lee, for their interest; Mr. and Mrs.
G. H. Tucker and Mr. and Mrs. B. L. Barrett for their
faith; and most of all my wife, Judy, for her love, belief,
and advice.

                    Archie P. McDonald
                    Stephen F. Austin State University
                    Nacogdoches, Texas

DAWN AT THE ALAMO
— Painting by H. A. McArdle (1836–1908)

Introduction

The Legend and
the Legend Makers

"TAKE care of my little boy. If the country should be saved I may make him a splendid fortune. But if this country should be lost and I should perish, he will have nothing but the proud recollection that he is the son of a man who died for his country." This passage from the second most quoted of the William Barret Travis letters was written on March 3, 1836, to David Ayers, who had custody of his son, Charles Edward. It suggests a compelling scene: the father-soldier, at a moment when every thought must be for his command, takes time to send word to his son's guardian, word that is full of hope as well as pathos. Knowing the worst, subsequent readers can easily identify with the small lad who is orphaned and in a strange and hostile land. They want to reach out a hand to steady him and to cheer the brave father who makes such a patriotic sacrifice.

It may not be wise to call attention to the part of the letter concerning a "splendid fortune". Rhetoric, it might be claimed, or perhaps poetic license, but no more than that, for Travis went on to talk about dying for his country. But it is exactly that aspect of Travis, the fortune conscious Travis, that it is hoped will be captured and appreciated in these pages. It is further hoped that we will emerge with a more human understanding of Travis. Some would call this purposeless debunking, but it really is a better way to appreciate him.

Travis is one of the most head-strong, high-stepping, opportunistic fellows to be found in nineteenth-century American history. All that most people ever know about this fascinating character is the whitewashed and degerminated man they encounter in seventh-grade Texas history, or see in one of the advertisements that are run each year in the newspapers and magazines during the week of the Alamo anniversary. This picture is usually of a mature man, handsomely attired in a waistcoat with tails, Wellington boots, a long sabre and a resolute look. He looks like a movie star trying to look like Travis. Ultimately this kind of image has to fade in the light of the truth, because Travis had a life before the Alamo that is as interesting as the story of his command there. While not as heroic or grand, knowledge of it is necessary to appreciate him as a man. It also rescues him from the limbo of a single act.

The "movie star" image lends itself to Legend, particularly the kind of legend that depends on just enough fact for permanence and general acceptance. But it is not above taking a little liberty with the truth. Most contemporary Texas history readers accept as gospel the information they find in the various biographical sketches of Travis. These sketches are often misleading because they are incomplete. Full of superlatives like "gallant," "brave," and "loyal," their creators use them to gloss either lack of information or indecision. These sketches usually have two major parts. First, birth to Texas (1809-1831), which gives the barest details of date and place of birth, parentage, and a word or two about education and religious background. A few go into some detail about Travis' marriage, and finish with a rhetorical question that wonders why he left it all behind and came to Texas. This question is usually left unanswered, and the entire story of his first twenty years is handled in a paragraph or perhaps a page. Part two of this saga recounts his involvements in the early fighting at Anahuac and at the Alamo. At this point few superlatives are spared in praise of the role Travis played at San Antonio, and of the "noble sacrifice" that he and the men made there.

Travis has emerged from this treatment as something of a historical curiosity. Nearly everyone in America has heard of him, but few know anything substantive about him. His place in history resembles a tropical hurricane which rises in the east from an unseen and unknown source, passes its time in relative obscurity until the moment when it becomes a full blown storm, then quickly blows away, leaving a vivid memory of its brief moment of glory.

Those who have searched for the historical rather than the legendary Travis find an abundance of the above described sketches which contribute to the Hurricane Travis analogy, but they searched in vain for a suitable biography. This is surprising because there are dozens of biographies of Sam Houston, David Crockett, James Bowie, Stephen F. Austin and others in the Texas galaxy. In addition, there exists good biographical treatments of far lesser personalities than Travis. There are several possible explanations for this absence of a good biography of Travis. First, the stem of the story, encompassing the years he spent in South Carolina and Alabama before coming to Texas, especially his reasons for coming to Texas, is shrouded in mystery and scandal. Second, an excellent treatment of Travis in academic thesis form was done nearly five decades ago, and several people who might have done competent biographies since that time were frightened off by its expected publication.

Still, the Alamo and Travis' role there has interested Texans and students of Texas history ever since it happened. Only three weeks after the fall of the Alamo, DeWitt Clinton Harris wrote to his sister in New York that "although the town of San Antonio has been taken by the enemy, our cause is going bravely on, the brave and gallant Travis, with his heroic men, held out to the last, and being engaged with superior numbers, their small force could not always stand the attack of the enemy. The

15

Mexicans succeeded in storming the place on the 6th inst. when Travis and his brave men fell sacrificed to the cause of liberty."[1] The attitude characterized by this appraisal dominated most of the memorials and reminiscences of Travis and of the Alamo throughout the nineteenth century and for the majority of the present century.

Some of the earliest objective research was done by Professor Samuel Asbury of Texas A and M College, now University. In the early 1920s he travelled to Alabama and South Carolina, the first Texas scholar whose tracks can be found there pursuing this subject, to collect materials on these important background areas. Professor Asbury's research did not produce a full biography. Within a few years, however, two theses written at the University of Texas did profit from Asbury's trailblazing. The first, entitled, "A Critical Study of the Siege of the Alamo and of the Personnel of its Defenders,"[2] written by Amelia Williams, set the tone of much subsequent writing on the Alamo. Lon Tinkle's *Thirteen Days To Glory*, published by McGraw-Hill in 1958, and John Myers' *The Alamo*, published by E. P. Dutton in 1948, owe at least some of their historical value to the previous research of Ms. Williams. Only Walter Lord's *A Time To Stand*, published by Harper in 1961, has really gone beyond the Williams model with fresh, perceptive research. Indeed, the publication of her study in some other form more available to the public would have rendered their works, other than Lord's, superflous, although each of these gentlemen brings considerable literary grace to their studies. The second, "William Barret Travis, His Life and Letters," written in 1930 by Ruby Mixon of Fort Worth, has remained the pace setter for Travisiana. Ms. Mixon's thesis is straightforward, and if a bit light on the early years, its conclusions are still largely valid. The real contribution of her work lies in the last three-quarters of the thesis, which is a collection of the correspondence and other papers relative to Travis. It contains nearly all the known Travis papers dealing with the Texas years.

Those who have written of Travis since 1930 have relied heavily on Williams or Mixon, or they have relied on someone else who has done so. This has meant that in the time since the Williams-Mixon theses were completed there has been little meaningful writing on Travis.

Surpassing everything else, at least in influence, has been the essay written by Joe B. Frantz for *Heroes of Texas*.[3] Professor Frantz, adhering closely to the Williams-Mixon theses, provides a modern if brief appraisal of Travis. His writing is not marred by the saccharine qualities that render many of the other "memorials" not only inaccurate but overly romantic. Frantz keeps his balance and produces a readable and reliable sketch for modern readers. Dorman Winfrey provided a biographical introduction for Robert E. Davis' edition of the Travis diary[4] that is similar to the Frantz model in form if not in style. Davis' edition of the diary is excellent, his research into the life of Travis for the period covered (1833-1834) is deep and inspired. He knows as much about the Travis of those years as anyone has ever known.

There are but three other items in the Travis bibliography that need to be mentioned. First, the longest and most detailed biographical attempt until recently was Virgil Baugh's *Rendezvous at the Alamo*, published by Pageant in 1960. It is subtitled "Highlights In The Lives of Crockett, Bowie and Travis," and it verifies its boast, if nothing more. Often unsupported by references and adhering closely to the Legend as well as selective parts of the Williams-Mixon theses, its greatest value is in the treatment it gives to Travis' Alabama years. There is a juvenile biography by Walter McCaleb, *William Barret Travis*, published by the Naylor Company of San Antonio in 1957. Most recently, Martha Anne Turner's *William Barret Travis*, published by the Texian Press in 1972, has appeared. Like the Mixon thesis, its principal contribution lies in its presentation of much of Travis' correspondence.

Others have researched the subject, but as of this writing these remain the principal publications on Travis. It is hardly an impressive list, considering the importance of the subject. There has been difficulty in obtaining materials on the early years, plus the territorial instincts of historians who sensed the eminence of a Mixon publication, but the reason seems to lie within the subject himself. Travis was an especially complex man. Unlike most of the others with whom he shared the stage of Texas history, he had no prior claim to fame and accomplishment. Houston, Crockett, Austin, even Bowie, were important men before the war and in sober moments expected to be important again. But this is not so with Travis; he was essentially unknown before the movement for independence and particularly the nature of his death brought him fame. He was also much younger, nearly twenty years younger, than any of these. His motives—for migration, for participation in the Texas Revolution, and especially for the Alamo decisions—are obscured by his death, and no public explanation for them was made while he lived other than in the politically oriented letters penned from the Alamo.

Perhaps the principal reason why a major biography has been so long in coming is the scarcity of materials. While he lived Travis enjoyed the anonymity of the frontier. He covered his tracks well, perhaps deliberately, so that one must wonder more at what has survived than weep at what little remains. In addition there are really three Travises, perhaps more. In South Carolina, where there are few records and no recollections, it is easy to talk of a red-headed kid who moved away while still a boy and later made something of himself. In Alabama there are more records and a few bad memories. Here Travis is remembered but not revered, an embarrassment more than a source of pride. The fact that he achieved some historical importance instead of getting himself hanged arches eyebrows and causes wondered surprise. In Texas, of course, there is the Legend and the attempts of the aforementioned writers to capture the spirit of Travis.

It is from this background that the present study has come; and in coming, it is hoped, it will have some relevance for today. There are certain ground rules by which this study has been written. First, it will attempt to appreciate Travis as flesh and blood; he was a very much alive young man with appetites and weaknesses as well as strengths and a sense of direction, a man who could appreciate and seize an opportunity rather than be simply the pawn of the events in which he was involved. It will attempt to be honest in dealing with the question of his legitimacy and the circumstances of his marriage, and with his motives for coming to Texas and of his life in Texas. On the other hand, it will attempt to treat the scandals realistically, this not for the sake of idle curiosity, but for understanding the man and his life.

Secondly, it will seek to evaluate Travis as a man of the American frontier. Too long he has been regarded only as a Texas hero, and as a personality of note in an important but unsuccessful mission. This is too limited. Travis was a central character, albeit a shortlived one, in a great adventure of the American frontier. His role, although small when measured against the more important careers of men like Houston, nevertheless played its part in the fulfillment of America's Manifest Destiny and the expansion of the United States to the Pacific.

Thirdly, it is hoped that this study will help give wider circulation to the facts of Travis' years in South Carolina and Alabama. Much is known about his life in Texas, at least as it appeared to the chroniclers of those times; yet the forces that made him the man he was lay far back in the States, in Carolina and Alabama, and these years are shrouded in much mystery.

Finally, after we have bared the story of this historical figure as well as we can, it is hoped that this study will provide a truer appreciation of Travis, for it is not by accident that we study him. There are lessons here for modern man, the kind of lessons we can learn and profit from through observing the mistakes of others, as well as those we may wish to emulate. Love him or hate him, call him saint or sinner, think of him as the Legend or something less, he deserves more than the fiction that most people believe to be fact. In the end, we will call him simply a man, or better still, just Travis, and accept him for that.

Top: *Saluda remembers her native son, William Barret Travis, with this monument erected between Saluda and Johnston on South Carolina Road 121.*   — Courtesy Saluda County Historical Society

Bottom: *The home of James Butler Bonham, Alamo courier, located not far from the site of Travis' birthplace near Saluda. The Saluda County Historical Society plans to preserve and restore this historic structure, important both to South Carolina and Texas.*
— Courtesy Saluda County Historical Society

1

South Carolina

MOVING was a natural thing for the Travis family. They
had been moving and setting up, then moving on again for
as long as there had been Travises. Always in the van-
guard of migrations and rearrangements, they seemed a
stable, hard working stock wherever they were, and not
just on the American frontier, but anywhere the frontier
was at the time. The earliest known member of the line
was among the invaders who came in the eleventh century
with William across the channel to conquer England.[1] In
the Battle Abbey Roll he is listed simply as Travers.
Travers established himself in Tulketh Castle, near
Preston, and became a part of the life of England. Travers'
self-composed epitaph in the Freery at Preston remembers
a bold man, one with the will to sire a bold line:

> I Travers by birth a Norman
> To gain victorious conquest
> With Wm. Conqueror in I came
> As one Chief rol'd among the rest . . . .

The Travers or Travis family, continuing the family
tendency for migration, was among the earliest to come to
Virginia. Edward Travers or Travis left the security of his
position on the Preston Guild for the unknown in America

in 1626 or 1627. Despite settling in Jamestown, a site that did not promise success, he seemed to do rather well and in 1637 married Anne Johnson. He received patent to land on Chipoake Creek and in time acquired considerable holdings in the area. In 1644 he was made a member of the Burgess from Jamestown, and by the time of his death had acquired extensive property. Virginia held the Travises for nearly a century before they followed the valley routes southward toward Carolina. It was somewhere in the century and a half between the family's living in Jamestown and moving to Edgefield, South Carolina, that Travers became Travis.

Not all authorities are convinced that Edward Travers was the sire of the entire American line.[2] The argument seems to hinge on the number of wives and children of Barret or Barrick Travis, the first of the family in South Carolina. The name William seems to be fairly common throughout the Travis family, but "Barret" or "Barrick" illustrates how names evolve on a moving frontier. Barrick Travis, the grandfather of William B. Travis, lived in Loudoun County, Virginia. In 1763, court records indicate that he was the indenture of Robert Watson and that he unsuccessfully sought to be removed from the obligation because he claimed that Watson abused their agreement. The court found against Travis, but when he was free he made the necessary preparations to move to Carolina. In August, 1772, he established himself on the Saluda River and petitioned the King's agents for 100 acres on the north side of the river, that was bounded on the northeast and east by land held by a man named Conniphan, on the northwest by land owned by one Weil, on the southeast by land owned by John Dooley. Vacant land lay on his other lines. His name is clearly spelled in the patent as Berwick Traverse.[3] The Berwick, after the English habit, was pronounced and later spelled Barrick, and that was soon shortened to "Barret." It is often written as "Barrett" even by members of the family; once William B. Travis spelled it so, and in the records of Edgefield County it is spelled "Barrot."

Barrick Travis moved his family into fairly wild country, although he was not the first in the region. South Carolina had been established much earlier, but the principal settlements were still on the coast, and the backcountry was largely unorganized. Roving traders and trappers, both French and English, had already penetrated it, but even they travelled paths long established by Indians. Beaver and deer hides had been brought from the region since 1690, and bears, wolves and wildcats were abundant. The Saluda Indians claimed the country, but occasionally other tribes, especially the Cherokee who lived mainly to the south and west, trapped its forests and streams. Gold traces more valued by the Europeans could be found in the white quartz which outcrops in the region. Granite lies beneath a soil that produced stands of hardwood alternated with pine and later green fields of upland, short-staple cotton.[4]

Among the earliest settlements in the region was Ninety-Six, which drew its unique name from the number of miles separating it from the nearest fort, Fort Prince George, or, as it was known by the Indians, Fort Keowee. Although individuals lived in the region around it prior to that time, Ninety-Six was settled in the late 1740s. They were mainly Scot-Irish migrants who came to the up-country as early as the 1720s. Indians occasionally caused trouble for these settlers, and Governor James Glen tried to ease some of the difficulty by establishing forts such as Fort Keowee and later Fort Loudon as close to the Indians as possible. These installations were really built to pacify the Indians, not police them. The Indians used them as trading centers and for protection, but the forts also subtly bound the Indians, especially the Cherokee, to the English. The French tried vainly to break up this cooperation to serve their own purpose of North American empire. The activities of such agents as Christian Priber were irritating, if not successful, mostly because Governor Glen knew how to deal with the Indians. In 1755 he travelled to Saluda, now called Saluda Old Town, to meet with the Indian Chief Conocautee, or Old Hop. Old Hop had refused to come to the governor, using as an excuse his fear of the white man's diseases, but Glen dealt well on his host's land, and on July 2, 1755, they agreed to the Saluda Old Town Treaty. The principal significance of the treaty lay in the fact that it solidified the friendship of the southern Indians and the English at a time when the French, using Indian alliances, were making their greatest effort to drive the English from America.[5] It was still English when Barret Travis arrived with his family in the early 1770s.

Travis survived rather than prospered in his new home at first, because those were hard times in South Carolina. He acquired sufficient land, but subsistence farming was about all that was possible, and the uncertain political condition which existed in the area for the remainder of his life probably held him below his potential; but when he died in 1812 he left a small legacy to his wife and children. He witnessed many changes in the region during his lifetime. When South Carolina joined the other colonies in revolution against Great Britian, she drew heavily on the western district for manpower. Captain James Butler led the principal group from the region, and most able bodied men served either directly in the army or indirectly through the many avenues available to them as guerrillas and suppliers. There was a post war economic slow down that also affected the back country. However, some of the memorable changes and events were happy, or at least were marks of recognition and progress. In 1795 Ninety-Six District was divided into counties, and the Travis family home ended up in Edgefield County, still frequently called Edgefield District. The community of Edgefield was designated the county seat in 1791, and court was commenced there the following year. A college was authorized for Ninety-Six, a name which persisted despite the legislative attempts to change it to Cambridge. Also a source of pride for the county was a visit in 1791 from President George Washington, who was touring the country. Although his impressions were uncomplimentary, he "honored" the county by mentioning it in his diary.

Travis' holdings changed in reflection of his fortunes. In 1797 he sold a parcel of land to James Wolf[6] and in 1802 he transferred 150 acres of his property on Mine Creek to his son-in-law Elijah Polk for $200.[7] Mark Travis, Barret's son, is listed as a witness to this last transaction, and an interested one he must have been because some of his own land was contiguous. Despite these liquidations, Barret Travis was still possessed of considerable property when he died in 1812. Since he had no will his estate was not settled until October 3, 1814. His wife, Anne, and his son, Alexander, were the administrators of the settlement. An examination of Barret's estate reveals much about the family's economic status. He left several head of livestock including 8 hogs, 17 head of sheep, 22 head of cattle and horses, and 46 geese. There were quantities of stored staple goods, including over 500 bushels of corn, two stacks of oats, and over 5,000 pounds of cotton. In addition there were wagons, gears, cotton cards, wheels, some furniture, standard farming tools, and most importantly, four men, and three women slaves. The total value of the estate, $4,232.12, was not an inconsiderable sum for the period. After debts and his wife's property were deducted, each of his children received $374.83.[8] Alexander and Mark Travis participated as the sons of Barret Travis, and their sisters were represented by their husbands.

Alexander and Mark were farmers, and they were already well established in the community. But they were very different in other ways especially in regard to religion. Shortly after the turn of the century South Carolina underwent a religious revival which was partially sparked by the visits of the wandering evangelist Lorenzo Dow. Many, including Alexander, were converted.[9] Mason Locke Weems had called Edgefield by the name of Pandemonium, meaning home of devils, and Alexander was among those called to change the county's reputation.

Alexander Travis was born on August 23, 1790 and was raised in Edgefield County on the family farm. He was noted all his life for his ability to labor long and hard. After his conversion in 1809, he was equally noted for his religious fervor. Shortly after his baptism at Addiel Church he was licensed to preach, and he served several churches in addition to continuing as a farmer before moving to Alabama. Despite his junior status Alexander became something of a family patriarch because of his religious leadership.

Mark Travis, on the other hand, was more earthy. Indeed, his activities have contributed to a uncertainty about the legitimacy of his eldest son, William Barret Travis. There are many legends connected with Travis' birth. Some are easy enough to explain; others are still unsolved. Mark Travis married Jemima Stallworth in the fall of 1807, and in the years they lived together produced eleven children. The eldest was William Barret Travis, who was born in 1809, and the youngest was James C. Travis, born on August 5, 1829. There is little agreement among historians or genealogists, however, about the exact number, about how many were boys and how many were girls, and under what circumstances the earliest child was born. Gossip, tradition, imagination, and possibly a little hypocrisy, have livened the stories. One of the most persistent stories yet the easiest to dispell deals with Travis' legitimacy. Another county tradition claims that France's Marshall Ney and Jefferson Davis were native sons. Topping that is the yarn that there was once a man named Travis who lived on Mine Creek with his wife, and, as they were barren, they longed for a child. Mrs. Travis, according to the tradition, often asked neighbors for one of their children, a practice not unheard of in frontier America. One morning when she went out to the cow pen to milk, she found an infant hanging in a basket on the bar, or rail, of the fence. The Travis' adopted the child, a boy, and named him Bar in honor of his method of coming into their home. Hence, it is suggested, the Bar or Barret that became William's middle name.[10] Actually Travis' middle name as written in the family Bible was simply "B." presumably standing for Barret, after his grandfather. There is a strong element of truth in this fence story, but it is either one generation off, or, if correct in time, only a tale used to ease the embarrassment of indiscretion. The locality of the Travis farm on Mine Creek is correct, and Barret Travis may have first married Elizabeth De Loach but is not known to have produced children by her. It is possible that this is how Barret Travis sired one of his sons. It is likely that this is the right generation but the wrong son, and is a yarn that Mark Travis told to explain his illegitimate son to the neighbors, friends, and family. Mark Travis appears in the family Bible as being born on September 6, 1783 at Cambridge, or Ninety-Six, which is in the wrong direction and too far away to fit the setting of the story. Like his father and his brother Alexander he was a farmer, and he did own land on Mine Creek, as well as other places, before moving to Alabama in 1818. Mark was, also like Alexander, a Baptist, but he never burned with the same passion as did his brother. Before his marriage, he was, according to his grandson, "something of a rounder."[11] A family version of the Bar story, not much talked about for obvious reasons but revealed to Samuel Asbury by Mark A. Travis in 1925, identifies this foundling as Taliaferro Travis, a natural son of Mark born prior to his marriage to Jemima Stallworth. He did not deny the child; instead he took him into his home and raised him. It is understandable that the eldest child of Mark and Jemima, William B. Travis, should become confused with Uncle Tol, as he was later known to the family.

Beyond the confusion of the fence story, there is also uncertainty about the birthplace and birthdate of Travis. One early historian placed his birth in North Carolina[12] another in Georgia[13], and one in Alabama[14], but most authorities accept the family Bible's testimony that he was born on his father's farm about four miles from the Red Bank Baptist Church near the place later occupied by the Bethlehem Methodist Church in Edgefield County, South Carolina.[15] The site is presently in Saluda County, which was created as a separate political district by the state legislature in 1897, and is located just off the road between Saluda and Johnston, South Carolina. A monument erected on the Saluda County Court House grounds commemorates the birth of both Travis and James Butler Bonham. Travis is possibly the most notable personage born in the area that became Saluda County, although ten of the State's governors and many of its federal and state legislators, prominent jurists, clerics and leaders, including Civil War Generals James Longstreet and Louis T. Wigfall, were from the parent county. Most place his birthdate within the first part of August, but at least one has set it as far away as April 9.[16] The principal disagreement seems to be between August 1 and August 9, 1809, although a newspaper account of the Travis family published in 1907 gave the birthdate as August 8, probably confusing William B. Travis with his son, Charles Edward, who was born on August 8, 1829.[17] The official genealogist of the Travis family, General Robert J. Travis, gives the date as August 1.[18] James C. Travis gave several statements regarding his brother in which he agreed with this date, and it is also accepted by Ruby Mixon, possibly because of James C. Travis' convincing testimony.[19] However, John Bennett Boddie, who saw the Mark Travis family Bible while it was in the hands of his grandson, Mark A. Travis, mentioned in a passage primarily concerned with the correct spelling and origin of his middle name that the date was August 9[20], and it is the date which Amelia Williams uses in "A Critical Study of the Siege of the Alamo And of the Personnel of its Defenders."[21] Most of the other Alamo scholars solve the problem by oblique references only to the year of birth or by ignoring it altogether. The weight seems to be in favor of August 1, although either of the dates, considering their closeness, is acceptable. Travis' age is of fundamental importance to much of his life story, but a difference of eight days is hardly crucial.

Growing up in the backcountry of South Carolina was hard for Travis. The babies came regularly after William was born, and there was always commotion and noise around the house. Sharing things with his older half-brother provided early companionship, and some sibling

28

rivalry as well. In his second year, the county was shaken by an unusual, but severe, earthquake. And the return of the country to war against Great Britain in 1812, although there was no fighting in their neck of the woods, caused disruption in the normal pattern of life. A pattern is necessary on a farm; there were always things that needed doing — ground to clear, crops to plant and harvest, livestock to tend — and Mark Travis undoubtedly anticipated the day that his sons would be old enough to help out. Summer's heat and winter's cold marked the passage of their infancy, and soon they were big enough to at least make an effort. Perhaps because of the circumstance of his coming to live there, few memories linger of Tol, but young William was noted in various ways. The discovery of James Butler Bonham, who first lived only four miles distance on the Charleston and Ninety-Six Road, would have added a new dimension to Travis' life. Bonham, pronounced Bónham in South Carolina, was Travis' senior by nearly two and a half years, but in later years he would be remembered largely because of his association with the younger man. The Bonhams were aristocratic people as such things were measured there. Immigrating from Maryland after the American Revolution, James Bonham married Sophia Smith of Mount William, South Carolina, obtained a place on the Saluda River, and became a planter. He played the role well. His youngest son, Milledge L. Bonham, became governor of the state in 1862, and James Butler, named for a local military hero, achieved fame also. The proximity of birthplaces and years of residence in the same area, plus the testimony of the Bonham family, are the strongest evidence that can be found for a friendship between William Barret Travis and James Butler Bonham in their boyhood years. It is deeply rooted in the tradition of the region, and is commemorated by a granite marker on the lawn of the Saluda County Courthouse. Walter Lord questions the validity of a Travis-Bonham friendship prior to their Texas meeting in the fall of 1835. He does not, however, prove that they did not know each other; he merely questions the relationship

29

because of a lack of specific evidence. On the other hand, Milledge L. Bonham claimed that "the lads appear to have been school mates, until Travis' parents took him to Alabama, about 1818."[22] Lord calls this Bonham family tradition. Despite their class differences, and despite the lack of specific evidence of a friendship here, it seems likely that the two would have known each other in South Carolina. Their youth would have prevented the depth of relationship usually suggested for them, but they were conceivably well enough known to each other for that kind of trust to develop quickly in the midst of the Texas crisis that awaited them.

Travis and Bonham might have met at church. The Travises, either from conviction or social commitment, were members of the Red Bank Baptist Church and both were frequently in attendance at its services. The Red Bank Church was older than Edgefield. It began with the preachings of the Reverend Joseph Reese of the Congaree Association near Columbia in the 1760s when Reese travelled the Saluda River region. His work stirred a few converts into establishing a shortlived church on Mine Creek in September, 1770. From this group the Red Bank Baptist Church was organized in 1784. The church, situated near a spring, was built on land donated by Robert Newport. The Reverend John Thomas was its first pastor and while the Travis' lived there, Red Bank Church's pulpit was also filled by the Rev. A. Norris and Rev. John Landrum. It was just before or during the time that William B. Travis attended Red Bank Church that a log structure was erected. A fine place for boys to gather while the older folks worshipped and visited, they could while away the hours when they were not actually listening to the preacher. The church was also a major part of the early education of both Travis and Bonham. There were no formal schools in Edgefield then; the country was too new to attract teachers, and those people who came had to earn their living from the soil like the rest. Still, there was time for boys to learn the rudiments of ciphering and reading from parents or preachers or anyone who had the time, and these early lessons served as good beginnings for both boys in another setting. For Bonham this meant fine schools on the coast, but for Travis it would mean a frontier academy and what amounted to self-instruction.

The country to the west came to be a favored topic of conversation around the Travis household in the years just after Grandfather Barret's death. For one thing, General Andrew Jackson had won significant victories over the Indians who had been checking the westward migration of many coast-bound Americans. The partial elimination of this impediment would not go unnoticed by the Travis clan, who had a penchant for moving anyway. But it was hard times in Carolina that caused them to be more than wistfully interested in the land of beginning again. The post-war years were not easy for back country farmers, and the declining price of cotton, coupled with the instability or failure of many small banks made a fresh start look particularly inviting. Beginning in 1816 and 1817, many Carolinians began the move to Georgia and Alabama. Uncle Alexander was the first Travis to go. In 1817 he sold his 500 acres — it could be called a plantation — to Reeves Martin for $2,200, and headed west. Crossing Georgia and pushing on into southwestern Alabama, he found a lush, green area that combined many of the best qualities of the Saluda River region and added a few of its own. It was wetter, and maybe a little hotter, but the timber was nearly the same, the same crops would grow there, and the ground was even the same reddish color in places. He stayed long enough to be convinced that this would be the new home ground, and in 1818 went back to fetch Mark and the others. Mark had to sell his own place and make other arrangements for changing his family's life so completely, including going to Red Bank Church on July 20, 1818 to get letters of dismissal for himself and Jemima.[23]

When all was in readiness the Travis clan set out for what was the last move for Mark but only the beginning of a life of many moves for his children. Young William was of two minds about the move. He was naturally apprehensive about leaving all that was familiar. But he was of an adventurous nature and in the end that side of him won. He was still too young to really understand why they were going, even if they explained it to him, and they might have had trouble expressing themselves other than in terms of dollars being lost there or to be made in Alabama. There were all of one mold, American frontiersmen with the itch to move on, to be in the thick of the action. The opening of the Alabama territory claimed many from the older, Atlantic states, and the Travis' moved with them. Their move was complete; although the family name is attached to avenues and parks and cemeteries in Saluda, no member of the family remained.

Behind was Carolina, ahead, Alabama. How could a boy better remember his ninth year than to be setting out on a great adventure.

Restored exterior of the William B. Travis home
. . . Perdue Hill, Alabama.
— Courtesy Joan F. Headley, Longview, Texas

2

Alabama

THE cane was thick, so dense that a boy seeing it for the first time would wonder if there was an end to it. A boy who had been on the trail for as long as William Travis had might well wonder if there was ever an end to anything. No specific account of the Travis' movements is extant, but they undoubtedly followed the same general pattern as did the thousands of others who were moving with them, and based on a general knowledge of American western migration, it is possible to speculate on the movements of the Travis family. At first it undoubtedly looked like a great deal of fun, and the excitement had made them think more about the going than the getting there. Now, he wondered, would they ever get there? All of their belongings were on the wagon, and William's mother and the younger kids rode on it too, sometimes. But since he was the oldest he probably walked, like his father did. When they started out the pace had been slow but it was nothing like now, for they were really anxious to get to the green Alabama that Uncle Alex was always talking about and praying over. The wagon was heavy with its load and the oxen were slow, but they got out of South Carolina before young Travis was able to realize that it was the first time in his life that he had been out of Edgefield District.

Moving across Georgia they saw many others who were making their way to the newly available Alabama lands. Some were not so fortunate as they were and did not have a wagon. A few had to carry what they could and forget the rest, and some put everything they could in a hogshead, ran a pole through it, and hitched an ox's harness to the pole. Young William Travis should have been glad that his family had a wagon, because that meant they could bring some furnishings and other things that reminded him of home. Home was the wagon now, and a rolling home at that. It was hardly ever in the same place two days running unless they had to wait for the road to dry after a rain, when the men needed to hunt, or when someone was sick. Usually they moved on every day, making camp around the wagon every night, and then they moved on again the next day. Travis probably liked the camp at night. After his part of the work was done and the oxen and horses fed and tethered, the canvas propped up on poles beside the wagon, and wood and water brought for the evening meal, he could watch his mother make the supper and wonder how she was going to make the corn meal any differently than it had been the night before. They undoubtedly went to bed early because it would take several hours to break camp again in the morning, and they would need as much daylight as they could get for travelling. Still, sometimes they must have been glad to sit up a little while extra and hear Uncle Alex talk about the Lord, or about Alabama. Somehow Alabama and Heaven blended together when Uncle Alex talked about them in the same evening.

The Travis family continued in this fashion until they reached the cane country. They travelled down the Federal Road, as it was called, a more or less continuous route from Greenville, South Carolina to New Orleans. The part they used had been cut in 1805 from Okmulgee in Georgia to Fort Stoddard; it was the principal route most South Carolina immigrants took to Alabama. When they reached the junction with the Mobile and Tuckabatchee trail, which cut sharply to the south from their

34

southwestern course, they headed toward the country Uncle Alex said was always green.[1] When they reached Alabama things got a little rougher. The settlers were more scattered, the road became a trail, and the grownups seemed to be much more alert for Indian signs. There were still Indians in South Carolina, and they were not altogether civilized either, but these unseen Indians seemed much more ominous. These factors combined to make the country harder to travel over and when they passed Fort Sepulga and began to draw near the area that Uncle Alex had visited the year before, they began to look around for a place to stop. Being Travises, they could not just live beside the trail as others did, but instead they had to push off laterally to the very edge of settlement near wild country. There were a few others in the area, of course, and because many of them had also come from South Carolina, they were known and were of assistance in acquiring land and establishing some kind of preliminary shelter.

When they finally stopped, the Travises were in Conecuh county, of late a part of Monroe County. The entire area had originally been a part of the Mississippi Territory, but in 1815 Governor David Holmes proclaimed the creation of Monroe County in honor of President James Monroe. Encompassing most of southwestern Alabama, Monroe County was soon chopped down by the establishment of other political districts, including Conecuh County, which was created in 1818. Even Conecuh was extensive, joining Monroe County on the west, Montgomery County on the north, Georgia on the east, and Spanish Florida to the south.[2]

Conecuh, or cane-land, from Creek language, was aptly named, and its density slowed but did not stop the persistent settlers who came to occupy and develop the land. There were few roads, no schools, churches, stores, and only the barest evidence of civilization when the Travises first arrived. Yet the land had already witnessed nearly two centuries of European exploitation. Beginning with the explorations of Hernando De Soto and continuing

35

through the fur trapping era, the thick timber had been a good cover for the animals and Indians and traders that used the same trails and paths. By the time the territory had been transferred to the United States—although mostly in isolated ignorance of the fact—it had also become a place of intrigue when the Spanish replaced the French as competitors for the Old Southwest. In 1788 a memorable tragedy earned the name of Murder Creek for one of the territory's principal waterways. How that name tingled the ears of newly arrived settlers when they first heard it. The imagination demands to know how the name originated, and the earlier comers liked to tell the johnny latelys that old Colonel Kirkland had visited the half-breed Alexander McGillivray on his way to Louisiana via Pensacola and had been led through the cane by one of McGillivray's mulattos. At the creek the party met a band of Indians and half-breeds returning from Pensacola; their leader was Istilliacha, or man-slayer. The band doubled back and murdered the Kirkland party in its camp, which was located along the creek. Only three blacks, including McGillivray's man, escaped to tell the story and to help name the stream Murder Creek.[3]

During the Creek wars General Andrew Jackson led his armies through the country, cut roads for his logistical support, and established forts, including Fort Claiborne on the Alabama River. It was to this settlement that the first Conecuh countians came. Alexander Autrey built the first of several residences on Autrey's Creek, not far from Murder Creek, and named the place Hampden Ridge. He was soon joined by Thomas and Eli Mendenhall, and Reuben Hart. More visitors and future settlers such as Alexander Travis came, and Conecuh was underway. In 1818 Alexander Travis brought his entire family from South Carolina, and they became bellwethers of hundreds more Carolinians and Georgians who followed. That year also saw the establishment of the area's first store, erected at Bellville settlement by Robert C. Paine, a half-brother to Mrs. Alexander Travis. It was little more than a building of pine poles that still had the bark on them, and the floor

36

was dirt, but it was a place to buy sugar, coffee and a few dry goods that were hauled in by oxcart.[4]

When Mark and Alexander Travis arrived in the fall of 1818 they located near each other for mutual protection and reciprocal labor. Still very different in personality, they were mindful of family ties and the need for each other's help in establishing new homesteads. Both were farmers, so their first thought was to acquire land. Later, when the land office was established for their area in Sparta, their squatter-acquired property would be in question, but now no one seemed to care if they took up a piece of unoccupied land. Their land was heavily timbered with hardwood, sprinkled with cedar and pine. The countryside was uneven, tending to a gentle roll, and the soil was reddish and thin with the rock never very far away. But it was still fertile from countless ages of natural buildup, a fertility that could too soon and too easily be worn down by poor agricultural techniques. The first job was to clear an area for a temporary shelter. Mark did this work himself because he had no slaves, but William and Tol were old enough to be of assistance. The first shelter was built by setting four corner posts about ten feet apart. Then two smaller poles were tied near the top, all the way around. William and Tol cut saplings which were then driven into the ground and set between the two small poles at the top, thus forming the walls of their first house. Their roof was the wagon canvas until it wore out; then anything that would work was used while they applied themselves to the preparations of the fields and a more permanent house. The floor of the first dwelling was dirt, but well-pounded it was quite firm, and could be kept surprisingly clean. The shelter—it was little more than that—held their few belongings and was a kind of rendezvous for a family that had to scurry about to keep alive. Jemima stayed at home base with the younger children, doing her cooking in the yard, while Mark and the boys hunted and got the farm started. The wagon had brought in all it could hold, yet there were few tools. An axe was essential for Mark to cut the timber and clear the land, and a grubbing hoe was useful in breaking the ground. Few in that country had shovels or plows, and most simply used a hickory stick to make planting holes for the corn seed that was brought from Fort Claiborne. At first the "fields" were quite small, looking more like latter-day gardens, but they represented much labor. The hickory stick-planter had the advantage of being easily replaceable, for there were few smithy tools for the repair or manufacture of metal implements. One of the greatest concerns was the lack of shoes. Those that had them conserved them for special occasions by going barefoot, but many had no choice. Indian style moccassins could be made from animal skins when necessary, but being boys, William and Tol did not mind going barefoot. They did mind the sameness of their diet. The meat on the table was dependent on Mark's hunting and fishing skills; often the wild foods were also used in season. But the staple ingredient of their diet was corn. They tried wheat first, but after a good start it failed as the land gave out and the rust came in; later on they grew corn because it was something for them and for the stock to eat. It kept for a long time after harvest, but sometimes it would mould; they ate it anyway. At first there were no grist mills and they had to crush the grain themselves with a sweep, but finally the force of the creeks was harnessed by mills and the corn was made into a meal.

After they had been in Conecuh a season or two and had the farm underway, it was time to replace the house. This time something more permanent would be built out of hewn logs. Others left the logs round and notched them at the ends to fit at the corners, but the Travises squared theirs, built it on sills, and roofed it with split boards. That kind of house can endure. Mark Travis lived there the rest of his life, and before he died in 1836 he acquired title to 200 of the surrounding acres and was thought of as prosperous. But the real success in Alabama among the Travises was Uncle Alex.

Alexander Travis thought of his coming to Alabama as a kind of special mission for the Lord. He had little training for the ministry beyond what his denomination termed "the call." He brought as his library only a King James version of the Bible and he matched that with a powerful drive for preaching. His kind were in demand on the frontier, and he worked as hard as he could to fulfill that demand. Frontier people were always in need of reassurance, and the emotional preachings of men like Alexander Travis gave them the reassurance they needed that God was in his Heaven but was willing to come to them with a helping hand if the drought lasted too long or the Indians turned hostile or some other calamity befell them. They knew that God helped those who helped themselves and they were always willing to do their share, but men like Elder Travis, as he was often called, helped to make things seem like they were going to come out all right. William Travis could not help being proud of his Uncle Alex as he watched him go about his work for the Lord. When they first came to Alabama, the Travises had lived together; but even after William's father had built his own place, William would come over often to visit with Alexander's family. All week long he would see Uncle Alex work hard during the day like the other red-dirt farmers, sweating in the Alabama sun to coax a living from the land, then sit up at night reading the Bible until after the others had gone to bed. Sometimes his only illumination was a burning pine heart, but he would stay with it until he felt that the Lord had spoken to him and had given him a message for the following Sunday. When the weekend drew near Uncle Alex would begin his preparations for travelling his circuit. It was not a real circuit like the Methodists had, but it was a circuit nonetheless, a regular pattern that he followed to meet the people who came out of the woods to hear the preaching, to be baptized or married, and to visit with the other people they probably had not seen since the last time he was around. Later, after William had grown up and gone off to Texas, Alexander Travis had a fine horse to ride on these rounds, and he kept up the circuit even after he became the regular pastor for several established churches. For a long time, however, William and the others would watch him start off on foot for his appointments—often times literally on foot because he would be carrying his shoes to save the leather if the weather was not too cold or the road too rough. He would also be carrying his poke—it later became saddlebags—and sometimes he would travel as much as thirty-five miles. Alexander Travis kept pretty much to this routine until his death in 1852. He was responsible for a considerable part of the religious and educational growth of southern Alabama. Nobody knows how many churches he helped to create, but Beulah Church and the churches at Bellville and Claiborne at least knew his influence. He helped establish Sparta Academy, as well as the town it was named after, and he was also responsible for the Evergreen Academy's existence. He even named the town it was located in because he said it was "forever green" there. More important to him, however, other than the regular Sunday morning preachings, was his being chosen for more than twenty consecutive sessions as the Moderator of the Bethlehem Association. All in all, Alexander Travis made his mark on his world, and he set a high standard for the rest of the family. William Travis was not always successful, but as long as he lived in Alabama he tried to live up to the expectations of his Uncle Alex, and William's youngest brother, James Callaway, called Uncle Alex "the best man I ever knew."[5] One reason for James' appreciation of his Uncle Alex was the way he saw others appreciating him. Known as the "peacemaker," his services were often sought in a kind of Solomonesque way to adjudicate the petty differences of neighbors, and only a Saint could do that regularly and survive.

William was growing older now, and staying in the little log house with all of Uncle Alex's family was a bit crowded; but when Alexander built his "big house" right in front of the log one, he could better enjoy his visits. The log house became a kind of utility building, and later, after Uncle Alex had put together a small fortune, it became a kitchen for some of the slaves. The big house was a typical farm dwelling of the period, but to William it was impressive. It had several rooms, even a parlor, and the floor was very fine. It was made out of nine inch boards set in with square metal nails. There was a secret stairway to the attic that only the family knew about because they still had to be prepared for Indian raids in that part of Alabama.[6]

Sparta was one of the towns Alexander Travis helped to organize. It was located a few miles to the west of his farm, and was founded to serve as a trading center for the area. This kept the settlers from having to make the long trip to Claiborne for their household needs, to market their produce, or to get their mail. But it was also created to fix a permanent place for the county court and as a seat of local government for Conecuh County. In 1819 the state legislature appointed Bartlet Walker, James Salter, John Speir, Radford L. Cotton and Robert Smilie as commissioners to fix a place for the county seat. Based on the information and the recommendation supplied by these commissioners, on December 3, 1821 the legislature situated the county seat in the southwest quarter of section thirty-one, township five, and accepted Sparta as the name for the place. It was supplied by Thomas Watts, a local attorney and a former resident of the town of the same name in Georgia. Not withstanding these coordinates, Sparta was actually laid out in the southeast quarter of section thirty-six.

Sparta grew rapidly. John Anderson and Abraham Blacksher were early merchants, a man named Gauf opened the first hotel, a pine-logged, dirt-floored inn, and John McLeod opened the first school. A courthouse and jail soon followed, as well as other stores and hotels, churches, and a Masonic Lodge, Euphemien Lodge No. 13. Most significantly for the development of the country, the federal congress established a Land Office in Sparta on May 11, 1820. The building where William Travis had the most business in Sparta was the Academy, the first real school that he attended. Sparta Academy was founded by a legislative act of December 8, 1821, and McLeod and later Murdock McPherson were early staff members. Travis' Uncle Alex was one of the trustees of the Academy, and this explains his attendance there. The money for the building was raised by a lottery and they prayed up the rest. Travis evidently took advantage of the educational opportunity that Sparta Academy offered to him. His adult correspondence is graced by good style and grammar, and his spelling is excellent when placed beside that of others of his day. At Sparta he learned some Latin and Greek, as well as mathematics.

When Travis exhausted the educational potential of Sparta Academy, he had to go to the neighboring Monroe County for more schooling. Although Sparta was a progressive, even prosperous community, its horizons were limited by its geography. Land-locked in a era that depended on water transport, no amount of road building to Pensacola and other water outlets could keep it abreast of communities such as Claiborne, which was better situated on the Alabama River. When Uncle Alex had to go to that community, William sometimes went with him, and on one of these visits he made the decision to seek his fortune in the larger town. He evidently decided early that the farming life of his father was not for him, for even after he came to Texas his land acquisitions were purely speculative. After he left his father's roof, he never once took to the farming life.

In addition to going to Claiborne with Uncle Alex for preaching service, William sometimes went there with Mark to get supplies or to sell his produce at the river landings. One trip he enjoyed making was to see the Count de LaFayette when he visited at Claiborne.

The town could be called a "boomer" town. Well situated at the high-point of navigation on the Alabama River, it was named after the fort constructed there by General Ferdinand L. Claiborne in November, 1813 as a base of supplies for his invasion of the Creek country. It was located high on a pine bluff overlooking the river, on the east bank near a place known in Indian lore as Lover's Leap. As a part of the Mississippi territory, the area was under the jurisdiction of Governor David Holmes and was a part of the region he designated as Monroe County. On

December 9, 1815, Fort Claiborne became the recognized county seat. The population by 1820 had reached nearly 2,000, up from 800 in 1817, and it peaked at about 5,000 within a dozen years, about 1830. The town lots brought a good price for both commercial and residential property, depending on proximity to the river. Coming up from the river was a sharp rise in altitude, and long slides were used to ease cotton and other produce to the water's edge for loading into the ships that came up the river from Mobile. Steps helped the passengers make the assent, and a road large enough to accommodate wagons was also available. From miles around, including the Travis encampment and Sparta, people came to take advantage of the commercial, social, and transportational facilities of the town. Claiborne housed physicians, jurists, and other professionals including journalists and clergymen, and it also had a Masonic Lodge and a school run by a man named McCurdy. A large Jewish population gave it a cosmopolitan flavor; and since it was in plantation country, there was also a touch of Africa in its streets. There was a race track, the usual saloons and gambling houses, and despite the reputation for ill health it acquired from periodic visitations of the yellow jack that came up the river on the flatboats and steamers, Claiborne refused to shrink from its potential. Naturally, when the civic leaders heard that such a notable personage as the Count de LaFayette, companion of Washington and still a hero to the backwoods Jeffersonians of the frontier, was touring the country, they hastened to put in a bid for a visit. On March 6, 1825, a committee met in the office of County Clerk James Draughan and selected James Dellet as their chairman for local arrangements. On the 21st, Dellet drafted the invitation to LaFayette, asking him to "touch" at their city on his way to Mobile. They would have liked to have had him for several days, but had to settle for a dinner and evening reception on April 6, 1825. After a tedious correspondence to keep both parties aware of the other's expectations, the anticipated day finally arrived. The General arrived at the lower landing and Judge Dellet delivered a warm, urbane welcome. LaFayette was conveyed to Gordon Robinson's house in William Henderson's carriage. The procession was led by the Monroe Cavalry and trailed by the committee, visitors, and "Citizens and Strangers." A bower eight feet long and fifteen feet wide was constructed for the public ceremonies. After the declaration of welcome, the party served a marvelous repast which included ham, turkey, roast pig, chicken, duck, roast beef, and mutton, all with the necessary trimmings, vegetables, pastry, and coffee. There was, no doubt, plenty of liquid corn available. An important moment for local Freemasons came when the distinguished visitor "took the East," or assumed the presiding officer's chair, and briefly addressed the lodge. A band provided dinner music and later music for dancing.

All this might have been a far cry from the entertainments of Paris for LaFayette, but for frontier Alabama it was a big event. They composed poems and songs to commemorate his visit, and even saved the sheets on which he rested. The Travis clan was undoubtedly in attendance. For a long time Uncle Alex had included the Baptist church at Claiborne on his circuit, and he certainly would not have allowed such an important occasion as this to pass without taking his family to observe it. The Travises had enough of Virginia and Carolina in them to stand in awe of the Great Revolution, and here was the man that they had heard so much about who had come from France to help out.[7] It would be a good time to take William Travis over anyway, because he was nearly sixteen and it was time for him to be about the business of finding his calling. Besides the matter of a profession, Claiborne offered other advanced educational opportunities. The year before several of Claiborne's leading citizens had petitioned the legislature to authorize the founding of Claiborne Academy for "regular and liberal instruction." In December, 1824 the legislature authorized the trustees to locate a site for the academy and to conduct a lottery for its establishment. It was probably with some reluctance that Mark consented for William to leave home for further schooling since he was now old enough to be of real help around the farm. But the father's pride, the son's ambition, and the uncle's insistence prevailed, and William Travis left home at the age of sixteen or seventeen. Except for visits, he never lived under his father's roof again.

A boy away from home had idle time, but there was plenty in Claiborne to occupy him. School was nearly an all-day affair, and there was the river and the activity of streets to observe and to keep up with. The Alabama brought the gamblers and preachers, fetched merchandise and hauled out produce, and a boy of middling years could spend many hours looking across that river and far beyond the other bank and wonder how far the world went in that direction. Coming from South Carolina at the age of nine had been his life's adventure thus far, but he was getting old enough now to look at the horizon.

For a while school and his calling occupied his time, and acquiring his own family settled enough responsibility on him to make him forget what lay beyond the other bank. First there was school. Travis did well there, so well in fact, that he helped out with the teaching of the others. This evolved into a regular position for which he was paid, and it became one of the several ways Travis hustled a living while he lived there.

Claiborne was still a hustling town itself. There were several merchandising houses, including Parks and Burke and Wm. Henderson & Co., and together the houses did a business estimated at two million dollars annually. There was cotton in the warehouses, and money to spend at Leonard Moore's hotel or Colonel Stephen Steele's jewelry store or at one of the three tailor shops. There were specialty shops and the work places of craftsmen and plenty of churches and doctors. Uncle Alex still supplied at the Baptist church and Travis visited with him often, at least until the local tanner, J. S. Schroebel, was converted and ordained and took over the church.[8]

The lawyers caught Travis' eye the most. There were several jurists in town, including federal Judge Tait and circuit Judge Lipscomb, and quite a few complimentary "judges," or practicing attorneys. They seemed to enjoy considerable prestige and to live fairly affluently, and Travis determined after a while that theirs would be his calling also. There is a strong probability that Uncle Alex had something to do with arranging for him to study law in the office of James Dellet, because Judge Dellet had lived in South Carolina at the same time they had and Travis knew him well.[9] There is some dispute over whether Dellet was born in Philadelphia or Camden, New Jersey, but most agree that he was born on February 18, 1787 and moved to Columbia, South Carolina when he was twelve. He was graduated from the University of South Carolina at Columbia, then South Carolina College, in 1810; and after informally studying law he was admitted to the bar in 1813. In 1818 Dellet was part of the South Carolina exodus to Alabama. He settled in Claiborne, a natural selection for a young lawyer who was eager to enter politics and make a name for himself. The following year he was elected to the first Alabama House of Representatives and became its Speaker. He served two other terms there, and after one unsuccessful race for a seat in the United States Congress he was elected to that body as a Whig in 1839. In Claiborne, Dellet was professionally and financially successful. When the town received its official incorporation in 1820, he was one of its three commissioners. He owned a number of lots within the town, and many hundreds of acres on both sides of the Alabama River. Easily the most prominent attorney in Claiborne in the 1820s, it was natural that Travis would select Dellet as his mentor.

Reading for the law was the accepted legal education on America's frontier. For Travis it also involved doing leg work and case reading for his teacher on the theory that he was learning by doing and that his labor was fair pay for the teaching. Later Travis established such a strong association with Dellet that he may almost be thought of as a junior partner, although the two men never struck a legal arrangement as such. Travis probably lived on the premises of Dellet's office, or possibly boarded in his home, a fine log house beside a spring that was a goodly distance up the bank of the river to the east.[10]

Working with Judge Dellet gave Travis contact with the community leaders, particularly the political officials. Sheriff George L. Medlock and Judge of the County Court Henry W. Taylor were friends of Dellet, and postmaster Samuel McColl handled so many of Dellet's business papers that it paid to know him and to court his favor.

There was one person in Claiborne that Travis was glad to know just for herself. While he was at the Academy he was about the same age as many of his students; in fact, he could have been their classmates at one time. A diary that Travis kept in Texas testifies to a strong interest in women, and this tendency was already evident. One girl in particular, Rosanna E. Cato, returned his attention. Her parents, like his, were backcountry farmers who had interests in Claiborne. After Travis became an attorney he often handled the legal business of her brother, William Cato, Jr., who was especially involved in local affairs.

Because of the ultimate breakup of the Travis-Cato marriage and the circumstances surrounding it, there is some justification for the rumor that their wedding was a matter of convenience. Still related in whispers, the rumor suggests only that "Travis became too familiar with one of his students and had to marry her." Considering the number of times similiar situations were repeated later in his life there is no reason to doubt it. If true, it also suggests an explanation for his jealousy at any attention she might pay to another man, even a friendly greeting. At first, they seemed happily married. He scrawled it in a Bible: "Married—on the evening of the 26th day of October, William B. Travis to Rosanna E. Cato."[11] The year, despite Travis' ommission, was 1828, and nine months and thirteen days later their first child, a son named Charles Edward, was born in Claiborne in the little house down from Dellet's where they lived. The cottage is still standing, long since coming to resemble hundreds of the other cropper shacks that abound in rural Alabama. Its single front entrance

47

flanked by two windows, a small gallery offered shade from the sun. A well just to the east was its water supply. Just how long Travis and his wife lived there is unknown, possibly for as long as he was in Claiborne. Part of the time, however, he practiced law across the river. There were many lawyers in Claiborne, and a new man in the profession had to beat the bushes for clients. Possibly supported by Dellet, Travis crossed the river and briefly maintained offices in Gosport, about six miles away in Clarke County. But the real activity being back in Claiborne, Travis would return as soon as possible. He had a fair business there, and Dellet's papers indicate that he was active in the affairs of the county. For example, there is a note from Travis to W. M. Abney for $150, one from Travis to L. C. French for nearly $200, and several cases in which he was an attorney are listed in the dockets of the Claiborne courts.

In 1829 Travis was only twenty years of age, he had been a teacher, and he was a practicing attorney. He also had a wife and child to support, and, as the legal business paid slowly, he was forced to broaden his activities. These activities reflected not only his needs but also his interests. First, he became a newspaper editor. Claiborne had been graced by the fourth estate since Tucker and Tucker had brought out the *Courier* in 1819, and the *Clarion* in 1820. These were followed by Christopher Dameron's *Gazette* in 1825 and by Thomas Eastin's *Alabama Whig* in 1827. In 1829 Travis issued the *Claiborne Herald*. He both edited and published it under the motto "Thou Shalt Not Muzzle The Ox That Treadeth Out The Corn." A subscription was four dollars per year, in advance, or five at the end of the year. It promised to "conspicuously" insert advertisements for one dollar for ten lines, and fifty cents for any continuance of the ad. Like most newspapers of its era, the *Herald* contained many advertisements that were really public notices of sales, legal transactions, and announcements of new businesses. One important service was a listing of unclaimed letters being held in General Delivery by Postmaster McColl. There were reprints of foreign and national news as well as local items. Travis continued to publish the *Herald* until his departure for Texas in the early part of 1831.

A second activity which may have been of some assistance to him in the community was his affiliation with the Alabama Lodge No. 3, Free and Accepted Masons, located at Claiborne. The Lodge had been chartered in 1819 by the Grand Lodge of South Carolina, but had participated with eight other lodges in 1821 in the constitution of the Grand Lodge of Alabama. The Lodge hall, whose lower floor was also the largest auditorium in town, was a hub of Claiborne's activities: it shared space at one time or another with the Baptist church and with the County government; it was also one of the buildings visited by LaFayette, a source of special pride to his fellow Freemasons. Travis had been many times within its walls on legal business, but when he approached it on the evening of June 29, 1829—apparently by dispensation since he was not yet the required twenty-one years of age—it was with considerably different feelings. No man has ever travelled East, as the Freemasons speak of this experience, without qualms. But Travis weathered it, as have most men who have gone that way before and since, and his quick mind served him well in the detailed memory work required of Entered Apprentice Masons. He was Passed to the degree of Fellowcraft on July 16, and Raised to the degree of Master Mason on August 13, 1829.[12] The lodge ceased to function shortly after Travis left for Texas, and the remaining members merged with other nearby lodges, but the old hall remained in Claiborne until it was moved in 1884 to Perdue Hill, a distance of only a few miles, to serve as a community center.

A third activity which may have been undertaken for business as well as personal reasons was Travis' commissioning on January 3, 1830, by Brigadier General John W. Moore, as Adjutant of the Twenty-sixth Regiment, Eight Brigade, Fourth Division of the Alabama Militia.[13]

These activities would seem to be those of a young man who was trying to establish himself in the community permanently. Hardly a year had passed, however, before Travis mysteriously burned his bridges and left for Texas. Going to Texas was different from going to Alabama. Alabama was within the United States owned territory, and its admission to the Union was obviously expected. Texas, on the other hand, was an uncertain country ruled by any of a number of temporary rulers of Mexico. Although American immigration had been tolerated, even encouraged during the 1820s, the uncertain politics in Mexico had produced caution. Finally official curtailment of immigration was pronounced by the Law of April 6, 1830. Texas had been for sometime, however, a haven for desperate men, men who valued its isolation because it was outside the United States and outside the influence of law, bill collectors, and if a man were careful, even his own memory of bad mistakes. One Alabamian expressed it this way: "I remember hearing the old timers of Claiborne and Perdue Hill say that when a man committed a crime, he fled to Texas as that was such a distant country he was sure the law would not pursue him."[14] Naturally not everyone who left the United States for Texas in those days was hiding a dark secret, but it is likely that many were as anxious to escape some kind of condition at home as they were to embrace new opportunity. Most people came for such a mixture of reasons that it would be hard to say more than that they were running from and to at the same time, and each could fill in the preposition as it most nearly applied to him.

Travis is unquestionably in this category. There are so many explanations for his going to Texas that the truth, like the circumstances of his birth, is difficult to learn. Ruby Mixon presents several unlikely stories, which she labels as such, and they need to be retold to demonstrate how far Travis legends range. First there is the tale that he went to Andalusia, Alabama one day, probably on legal business, and while his horse was tied ouside his destination some prankster cut off its tail. When Travis discovered the vandalism he was so enraged that he vowed he would not live in a state where such acts were committed, and he mounted his disgraced steed and departed for Texas.[15] Another story is that Travis was on the losing side in a political dispute to determine the seat of Clarke County, and he was so disgruntled by defeat that he left the state. These stories rank with the laudatory biographical sketch explanations that he was "drawn by the spirit of liberty that was being tested in Texas" or that he was swept along by the force of the frontier. All of them are inadequate, insufficient, and at least partially inaccurate explanations. This is not to say that he was not sometimes politically unhappy, or that he did not suffer when pranksters were around, or that he did not love liberty, or that he denied opportunity. There was something far more important than any of these things that precipitated his departure. And it was something that was very personal.

Since the beginning of their marriage the Travis' had appeared happy, but underneath the surface there was a growing uneasiness. Perhaps they were too young, but then many marriages contracted at their ages were successful. Perhaps there was not enough money, but Travis obviously worked hard to provide. Perhaps the first child came too quickly and they had too little time for getting acquainted. Probably it was that Travis knew too much about Rosanna before they were married to trust her afterwards. There is no proof that she was unfaithful to him, but there is ample evidence to suggest that he was of that opinion. His brothers suggest that he had "to put up with a lot," but this may be dismissed as family loyalty and the fact that they would have been too young to have judged. Certainly Rosanna's brother believed her innocent and came to feel that Travis had simply deserted her. The truth is often difficult to determine; thus what men think is true is what dictates their decisions. And Travis thought that Rosanna was unfaithful to him; he even suspected that the child she announced she was carrying in the winter of 1830 was not his own. He had been a good father to Charles Edward, caring for him as an infant and in later years providing him with a guardian, but he did not even wait to greet his daughter when she was born on August 4, 1831.

51

By then Travis had been in Texas at least three months, and he had been gone from Alabama longer than that.

The circumstances of his departure are vague, but a clear enough picture can be formed from the several statements made by family members and by residents of Alabama who knew him. Although some contemporary Alabamians dismiss the stories of Travis' reaction to his wife's alleged indiscretion as "Texas stories," they did originate in Alabama and have some basis in fact. What seems indisputable is that Travis killed a man because of his wife's amourous involvement or suspected involvement and then quit the country for Texas. The circumstances vary with the teller, but all agree on this much. First, there is the statement of Ed Leigh McMillan of Brewton, Alabama.[16] According to McMillan, who gathered his information from Travis' relatives and others, the story involves intrigue, late night meetings, and much drama. In a meeting of the Circuit Court in Claiborne sometime during 1831 a man was tried for murder. Both the defendent and the deceased were referred to as "typical men about town," and at least one and perhaps both were gamblers. They had quarreled on numerous occasions, and the dead man had often been threatened by the accused, who had been seen with him shortly before he was found dead. Travis, according to this version, was a constant and very interested spectator at the trial, and when it became apparent that the man was going to be convicted, he hurried home to pack his bags, got his horse ready, and under cover of night sought an audience with the presiding judge. From him Travis secured a promise, possibly under a misuse of Masonic law, not to reveal until morning what he was going to say. He then confessed that he knew the accused to be innocent because he had committed the crime himself when he had learned of an affair between the man and his wife. The understanding judge sent Travis on his way and acquitted the wrongfully accused defendant.

A slight variation is that the murdered man was an Alabama River gambler who called upon Mrs. Travis, perhaps frequently, in Travis' absence, and the situation became the talk of the town. With the assistance of one of Judge Dellet's slaves Travis lured the man into a vulnerable position and killed him. The next morning one of Dellet's slaves, possibly the same one, announced the discovery of the corpse and then found himself accused of the crime. At the ensuing trial Travis was his attorney. When he found that only his own confession could free his client, he sought a private consultation with the judge, who, in this version, was also Dellet. Once he had admitted the crime and incidentally saved his benefactor's valuable slave investment, the judge gave him three choices: he could remain silent, and thus insure his own freedom and his client's conviction; he could confess his crime and accept the consequences; or he could make a full confession and then go to Texas, thus allowing both men to escape prosecution.

A more direct version, and one which appears more likely, is found in a statement by Phillip Alexander Travis, William Travis' nephew. In this story Travis simply sought out the man, a river gambler, who had offended his home, and shot him down. When he appealed to the "unwritten law" there was no legal repercussion, but he felt that his name and practice had been so adversely affected by the incident that he left Claiborne for Texas and a new life. All versions agree that when Travis left he was accompanied by a body-servant named Ben, and most have it that it was this same Ben, who, after five years of adventure in Texas, returned to Alabama to bring the news of his master's fate and to bring home some of his belongings to the family.

What emerges from these stories and the behavior of Travis in Texas is this: the Travis marriage had been rocky from the first; William at least suspected and perhaps even had concrete evidence of his wife's infidelity; and he slew the correspondent, who was then appropriately buried in an unmarked grave in the Jewish cemetery. There may or may not have been a hearing, perhaps there was even a trial, but Travis accepted the responsibility for his act and simply left by public tolerance. It is possible, even probable, that he intended to bring his family to him once he had established himself in Texas. Certainly Rosanna and her family anticipated this, as is evidenced by her letter to Judge Dellet in 1834 when she sought his assistance in securing a divorce.[17] She professed then to have confidently expected Travis' return or his summons, but also modestly claimed ignorance as to his reason for leaving in the first place. This may be excused as modesty, because Dellet would surely have known the circumstances. But there is considerable sincerity in her words when she speaks of his long expected return. It is possible that he was deceiving her in this for some purpose of his own, perhaps spitefulness. His diary testifies that he was not lonely in Texas even while he carried on a fairly brisk correspondence with Rosanna and her brother William.

Of all the local stories about Travis' departure, the one that is most appealing to the adventurous spirit is told by Raymond Fountain of Monroeville, Alabama, who got it from his father, a close associate of the Travis family. Travis, it suggests, simply killed a man who offended him, did not need to make much of a public announcement or confession because everyone there knew who committed the crime and why, got on his big black horse ("my Daddy was a hoss man and he say it was sixteen-hands high"), jumped him into the "rivah" and disappeared. No one knew where he went until they heard about the Alamo. Why did he kill the man? It was a lawsuit, it involved something he did not want talked about. What? (With dropped eyelids) Something about somebody's wife.

Discretion looms large in rural Alabama.

Just twenty-one years of age, Travis left a wife, a son, an unborn daughter, a legal practice and an established life and headed his "big black hoss" for Texas. If there were any lingering traces of boyhood in him the experiences of the last two years in Claiborne varnished them over. He was a man now, full grown, but alone and adrift. As he came up the west bank of the Alabama, as he had done so often in the past when going to Gosport, he reined up for a last look at the crossing, and up the bank to the buildings and in his mind's eye to the little house where his family lived. More than the river lay between them now, and soon the miles to Texas made the breech wider and wider until it was uncloseable. His thoughts must have wondered to many things. Even through the hurt of his own loss and sense of pride he could remember some good times, perhaps going back even to being a boy in Sparta, and going to preachings with Uncle Alex, or even farther back his boyhood experiences in Edgefield. William Barret Travis was a long way from where he started, but he was going farther still.

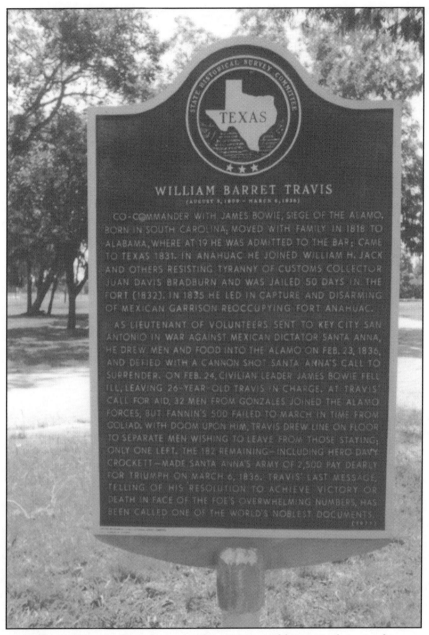

*Texas Historical Marker erected in 1971 at Old Fort Park in Anahuac
to highlight Travis' role in the 1832 and 1835 disturbances there.*
— Forest View Historical Services

3

Anahuac

The journey westward from Claiborne through eastern Alabama went well. It took Travis through familiar scenes of thick woods, red-dirt road banks, and houses and other surroundings that were well known. Gosport, where he had practiced law, was only a few miles and was reached easily. But gradually the country became less familiar, more interesting, and more demanding; so the farther he went the less he had to think about what he had left and the more he could dwell on what lay ahead. Going west was not exactly new for Travis. Although it had been more than ten years since the family had moved from Edgefield to Conecuh County, that had been the great adventure of his life and it was easy enough to remember, even now. For him the view was usually forward anyway, and he and the horse just naturally headed in the direction that most other Americans seemed to be going. This was different from the last move, however. Then it had been with his parents and his brothers and sisters. He had left behind all that was known and secure as far as friends and familiar places were concerned, but he had then been in the company of relatives and he had the promises of Uncle Alex to ease any youthful doubts. Now he was alone, completely alone, and he had to struggle with that and with the thoughts of Rosanna and Charles all by himself.

There is no way to know what Travis' thoughts were as he rode along. A romantic suggestion is that he pined away the miles with his heart broken and his mind numbed by sorrow. But this hardly fits the pattern of behavior he established in Texas. He was reckless there, carefree even, and he seemed to impose needless danger upon himself. But he seemed always to be going forward, to have a goal, an image of success that was framed by wealth, prestige, and peer acceptance. Still, he must have thought of Rosanna. Not knowing, or perhaps even caring, if he would ever see her again, the magical camera of the mind's eye could still produce an instant picture of the dark, wide eyes, the long angular nose, and the thin mouth that creased a prominent chin. Strong chin, strong personality. Two strong, even intolerant personalities. These memories would go into his baggage, too. Rosanna was a handsome woman. In the fashion of the day her dark hair was parted in the middle and piled on her head, revealing a long neck and a full bosom that narrowed considerably at the waist.[1] There were many women in Texas who would help blur the picture and erase some of the memories, but she was his first, and the first is not to be forgotten.

Travis could not have ridden far without having to make a decision as to his route. There was never any question about where he was going—"G.T.T." was the slogan of the southeast—but how he would get there did have to be determined. Having lived in a river port, the logical course would have been to go down the Alabama to Mobile, then overland or by coastal boat to New Orleans, and then by schooner to the Trinity or the Brazos in Texas. But Travis did not do that, at least not all of it. He left riding a horse, heading west. He may have taken some kind of vessel at the Tombigbee or at least at the Mississippi, and then gone on to Texas via New Orleans. Another possibility is that he continued overland to Natchez, crossed there at an established ferrage, and continued through Louisiana to Natchitoches, another established trading post with a long history of outfitting travellers who were going to Texas. From Natchitoches he could have retraced the steps of the Frenchman Louis Juchereau de St. Denis, the first European to blaze a trail westward into Texas. This was the same route followed a century later by Moses and Stephen F. Austin and hundreds of others. This trail would have brought him through Nacogdoches on a southwestward course that would have taken him directly to Austin's colony.

This latter course seems most likely, since it is at San Felipe de Austin that Travis' first documentable appearance in Texas is made. There on May 21, 1831, Travis made his note to Austin for a title to land. The language of the note reveals that he had already been admitted to the colony as a settler. His note was for ten dollars, but it promised an additional forty dollars at the end of one year.[2] In his statement before the Registrar of Families, S. M. Williams, Travis was listed as applicant number 578. He recorded his name as William B. Travis, age as 22 years, and station as "single." This merely could have meant he was travelling alone, but it is just as likely he covered his past by lying about his wife and children. He did testify that he was from Alabama and that his profession was the law. The date of arrival is simply May, 1831.[3] The land for which he applied lay adjacent to and south of a tract owned by a William Vince.

It is possible that Travis took the water route and landed at Anahuac, near the upper end of Galveston Bay and not far from the mouth of the Trinity; then he could have proceeded to San Felipe, the nearest seat of government. If he had gone here first, however, it is very likely he would have been detained along with other illegal immigrants and would have been involved much earlier in a controversy with the military commander there. He would call both San Felipe and Anahuac home for the next few years as he shuttled about the country in the legal profession. While at San Felipe he stayed usually at the hotel run by Jonathan C. Peyton and his wife. Here he met Robert M. ("Three-Legged Willie") Williamson, and other prominent or rising frontier lawyers.[4] Regardless of how he got to San Felipe, it was easily discernible that there was a surplus of "lawyers" there, and that the establishment of new ones who were uninstructed in the differences of Latin legalism from their English background would be difficult. Anahuac, on the other hand, was just getting started and would offer more opportunity for a struggling lawyer. Quite probably Williamson recommended such a move to many young settlers, because Travis and Patrick C. Jack made the move to Anahuac about the same time and their careers there were intertwined for quite some time.

Anahuac was of relatively recent origin. There are several suggestions about how it received its unusual name, most of which deal with its proximity to water. One explanation holds that it was named for an Indian chief, An-aw-ha, whose name meant "plain near or on the water."[5] Another claims that it is of Aztec derivation, was originally the name of Mexico City, and was borrowed for another settlement near to water.[6] The town was established in 1821 as a port of entry for American settlers coming into Spanish territory. It was for a time called Perry's Point, for Henry Perry, but was changed to Anahuac by the time a Mexican garrison under the command of Colonel John Davis Bradburn was stationed there in 1830 to enforce customs and colonization restrictions. The community was situated at the northeastern corner of Galveston Bay, then sometimes called Trinity Bay, on a bank that rose about thirty feet from the waterline. It looked out onto a body of water that spread for twenty miles across and approximately sixty miles southwest to Galveston Island. It was located near where the Trinity emptied into the bay, which gave it certain navigational advantages that were still hindered by bars which blocked the river's entrance to the heavier vessels. A traveller visiting there on March 26, 1831 reported sighting from fifteen to twenty log houses and huts, seven "poor shops," with the community dominated by the barracks for Bradburn's garrison. His headquarters were located at one end and the guard house was at the other.[7] The settlement was located on a bluff near the water, but the country immediately north was thickly covered with timber and undergrowth, not unlike that which Travis had been accustomed to in Alabama. To the east and west the land was flat and open and could accurately be called a prairie, but to the north it was timbered, first in pockets or islands surrounded by prairie, but it gradually thickened until it became a part of the great East Texas forest or Big Thicket country, a place to be avoided because of its density.

The area was sparsely settled with American immigrants being the most numerous. Despite the years of ownership by the Spanish and the Mexicans, these nationalities were largely unrepresented except by the garrison at Anahuac. When Travis arrived the most prominent settler in the region was James Taylor White, a cattle raiser, who had more than 3,000 head of stock in 1831. The country around Anahuac was varied in its kinds of timber resources. The larger stands were mostly pine with cypress predominant on the river banks and in swamp areas, and the flat lands were sprinkled with cedar, ash, pecan, and oak, walnut, and locust. There were also dense canebrakes that were virtually unpenetrable. The open lands would produce fair returns of corn, cotton and even some sugar cane. The woods and prairies abounded in wildlife. With seasonal variance ducks, pelicans, cranes, eagles, hawks, buzzards, and wild turkeys were present, and the deer were so numerous they often herded. The woods contained wolves, bears, foxes, raccoons, squirrels, wild boars, and up in the Thicket there were also panthers, or wildcats. Acquatic life in the form of red, buffalo, cat, drum, perch and other fishes, as well as oysters and crabs, was numerous. The alligator was easily seen and quite large.

Such a country was made for Travis. It offered him isolation if he had any lingering apprehension about Rosanna and the Alabama River gambler; it offered a place to start again in the legal business where the competition was not quite so keen; it offered reasonably familiar surroundings; and above all, it offered the opportunity to make a name and a fortune rapidly. He was soon prowling the country looking for land.[8]

Whatever his motivation he planned in a grand style. In November, 1831 he asked Austin for a recommendation to become the American consul for the Texas coastal area. On November 25 Austin wrote to Thomas Hart Benton, senator from Missouri and a promoter of western expansion, to recommend the bearer, a Mr. W. B. Travis, who probably would apply for an appointment as "U S consul for the Harbor and Bay of Galveston in Texas." Austin admitted that his personal acquaintance with Travis was brief, but claimed that he was recommended to him by persons of respectability and "I can with full confidence say that he has acquired the esteem and respect of the better part of the people in the section of the country where he resides which is on the head of Galveston Bay, and I have my self no hesitation in recommending him as a suitable person for the appointment of Consul—."[9] Travis apparently did not press his claim, but the letter does indicate that he had already taken up residence in Anahuac by the fall of 1831 and was seeking to expand his influence. Dr. N. D. Labadie, a merchant and physician at Anahuac who arrived on March 2, 1831, subsequently mentions in his account of the disturbances of 1832 that Travis and Jack arrived sometime after he did to make their home there, to improve themselves in the Spanish language, and to learn the laws of Mexico.[10] It is therefore probable that Travis established himself in Anahuac sometime in the summer of 1831. Apparently by autumn he felt himself proficient enough in both the Spanish language and law to serve as a consul. Even if he had secured the appointment it is problematical whether or not the military commander there, Colonel Bradburn, would have received him.

The Bradburn disposition, and indeed the entire story of the Anahuac disturbance which occurred in the late spring and early summer of the following year were important to Travis' development as a prominent figure in Texas. Yet it is easy to lose him in the story, despite the fact that he was

62

such a prime mover in a part of the action. The explanation is simply that he became active in the disturbance after it was already well under way, and in fact, it would have happened without him. His involvement illustrates his knack for finding controversy and positioning himself so as to benefit from its result. It is entirely possible, owing to his late arrival at the place, that he did not fully grasp all that was at stake, how deeply rooted was the unhappiness, or how swift was the crosscurrent of differing political and cultural viewpoints.

Long before Travis came to Texas, the forces which produced the events of the "disturbances," or the revolts of 1832, were at work.[11] They include the internal politics of Mexico, with federalism and centralism as polar positions; the differences between civilian and military agencies of government; the long-standing apprehensions on the part of Mexican officials regarding the designs of the United States on their northern holdings, especially Texas; the ideas and interests of American developers, especially the shaky, highly-speculative ones who desired greater latitude to bring in more setters; the desires of the already established settlers who wished to retain such institutions as slavery and avoid unwanted taxation; the understandable differences in cultural backgrounds; and, finally, the personalities and aspirations of many individuals, including Bradburn, the customs collector George Fisher, General Manuel de Mier Y Teran, and of course the Anahuac settlers and their other colonial support. Ruby Mixon claimed for Travis a "more or less obscure and passive position in these events which finally centered about him and his friends."[12] This is a marvelous insight into the situation as far as it goes. The next and obvious step, however, is to marvel also at his ability to become involved in an already explosive situation and increase the tension in such a way as to become its central, and sympathetic, character.

To understand how Travis was able to do this, and to explain the difficulties of 1832, it is necessary to briefly examine the background of American colonization in Texas prior to Travis' arrival. Spain's original claim to Texas provided that nation with a vast and beautiful land. Unfortunately for Spanish interests, its beauty was largely surface, and as far as their technology was able to learn it contained no deposits of gold or silver. Its value was, therefore, essentially negative. They did not want anyone else to have it because its emptiness gave them a comfortable buffer from other European penetrations into the more southerly lands that had intrinsic value for them. First French and then later American trespasses had drawn a number of military expeditions into the country to defend it, usually with severely punitive results. Missions that were established earlier in the Spanish experience were either abandoned or greatly reduced beyond San Antonio, and they relied on harsh punishment of offenders to deter illegal entry. Still the North Americans advanced, and in the latter part of the eighteenth century the Spanish flirted with a conspiracy to lure some Americans into Spanish lands. Promises of large land holdings and wealth—the dreams of empire—it was hoped, would lure them in to be used as a block to American westward expansion by conquest. But in the 1790s Napoleon reclaimed the land from a weakened Spanish government, the European interests of Spain became involved, and they were forced to surrender the significant strip of their lands in the Mississippi Valley to France which was later purchased by the United States. Then in the first quarter of the nineteenth century, a national spirit in Mexico was enflamed. A series of revolutions, which, combining with Spanish weakness abroad, succeeded in establishing an independent Mexico. The political nature of the new republic— centralist or federalist—would be important in the next phase of the story, the coming of North Americans as permanent residents.

The earliest arrival of North Americans in Texas is undocumented. American frontiersmen disregarded international boundaries either through indifference or ignorance and pushed on to whatever called them—fur, adventure, the horizon—or whatever drove them—the law, debt, or failure. But shortly after the turn of the century, their invasion became more structured. The title "filibuster" can be applied to these more or less organized penetrations. The first was led by Philip Nolan, who was unofficially sponsored by General James Wilkinson, United States frontier military commander in the Southwest. Nolan was ostensibly a mustanger, but his mission was to determine the ripeness of Texas as a plum for the United States to pick. In any case, he was met with the traditional Spanish reaction to invaders; he was captured by a Spanish patrol and killed in a skirmish.

The American-Texas frontier remained tense for some time. In 1806 Wilkinson met with General Simon Herrera, his Spanish counterpart, and arranged a temporary military solution to what was essentially a diplomatic problem. They called the area between the Sabine River and the Arroyo Hondo, a tributary of the Red River, a neutral ground, and agreed to withhold troops from the area so as not to arouse suspicion of invasion. This unpoliced strip attracted an immigrant population that was troublesome, and by mutual consent Lieutenant Augustus Magee led a clean-up expedition into the area. Magee did his work thoroughly, but he was captured by the geographical manpower potential of the area; when he encountered promotional difficulties within his own army, he united with a Mexican revolutionary, Bernardo Gutierrez de Lara, in still another filibustering invasion of Texas. His fate was similar to that of Nolan, although the method of his death is questionable.

The border difficulties were seemingly settled by the signing of the Adams-Onis treaty between the United States and Spain in 1819, but the solution was more apparent than real. The forsaking of the lands west of the Sabine by the United States denied the yet unnamed but very real American dream of Manifest Destiny. Call it land hunger, greed, or national interest, there were many strong-minded men in the Southwest who were unwilling to accept this national self-denial. Natchez was a center of such sentiment, and from there Dr. James Long came in

1819 to claim the empire that awaited beyond the Sabine. Long's dreams were unfulfilled, but his two expeditions sustained two related ideas: regardless of treaties signed by the United States, the adventurous Southwesterners would not be denied their expansion, which was tied to their attitudes on the extension of slavery; and the continued violation of their territory by such Americans further convinced the Spanish, and soon the Mexicans, that their lands were still vulnerable and were probably the object of an American conspiracy.

Considering these invasions it is a wonder that Moses Austin received the courtesy he did when he travelled to San Antonio to seek permission to colonize a portion of Texas with North Americans. Austin, himself a persistent migrant, had followed the mineral frontier from his native Connecticut to Virginia and then to Missouri, where he was a resident-citizen when the Spanish had been forced to cede Louisiana back to France prior to its sale to the United States. The Spanish king promised at the time that any of his subjects who wished to remove to other provinces under his authority would continue to enjoy that prerogative, and recent reverses with his investments, particularly in banks, had forced Austin, despite his advanced years, to once more seek his fortune by moving west. Austin unfortunately died before he could realize his last dream, but the standard was assumed by his son, Stephen Fuller Austin, one of the greatest promoters in American history. Austin's interest in Texas was at first mild, really more natural concern for the endeavors of a parent. It became an obsession. At first, like his father, seeking fortune, he eventually sublimated nearly every personal interest to the success of his colony. His road was often rough. His first contact had been with the Spanish, but the struggles of the Mexican nationalists proved successful just at the moment that he had won Spanish acceptance, and many more days of labor had to go into securing the approval of the new regime. At last he was about the business of selecting a site for his colony, establishing its headquarters at San Felipe de Austin, and

66

admitting the carefully screened colonists who were to populate his enterprise. But others came too; some, under empressarial sponsorship, with permission, and many without it. And as they came they increased the anxiety of the successive Mexican governments over the immigrants' intentions, and even more the intentions of the United States.

Changes in Mexican law complicated the relationship. Originally a single, indivisible republic, at least in name, Mexico adopted a constitution in 1824 which created a federal government. Texas was linked to Coahuila, the region immediately south of the Rio Grande, and the state government was given charge of immigration and land alienation. In 1825 the legislature enacted a colonization law that was remarkably liberal in its provisions. Additional empressarial grants were extended, and land was available to virtually anyone who applied, so long as he was willing to become a Mexican citizen and give at least some token of being a Catholic. Many were able to avoid, rather than evade, even these regulations by the sparsity of settlement and the lack of enforcement. But the more the immigrants came to take advantage of these opportunities, the more some Mexican leaders worried. The Fredonia Rebellion, centered in the Nacogdoches region, and the two attempts in the 1820s by the United States to purchase Texas were taken as evidence that the North Americans' interest in Texas was acquisitive and would ultimately be prosecuted by some overt venture. The internal politics of Mexico also played a part. The persistent competition between centralists and federalists in Mexico had ramifications for a colony that was different in every particular from nationality to cultural-legal arrangements, and where the natural sentiments would be for home-rule. Yet many of the provincial agents with whom the colonists had to deal, particularly in the military sphere, were centralists at heart. And the latter were most concerned at what they believed to be either a natural evolutionary or a potentially revolutionary movement in Texas. General Manuel de Mier y Teran, military commander of the Eastern Interior States, had charge of the area. Teran was faced with a difficult task. With insufficient troops and inadequate financial support for even the few he commanded, he had to guard and police many hundreds of miles of territory which was peopled by his own kind, by Indians, and by an increasing number of North Americans. And he had to deal with a civilian state government which shared jurisdiction with him but which was often at cross purposes with his centralist assignment. His worst error in this trying job seems to have been in the selection of men to represent his authority, particularly at Anahuac and Galveston, but this may be as much testimony to the nature of his manpower reservoir as it is to his ability to judge men.

Teran's problem seemed to be linked to the swelling numbers of Americans in his province, who, despite their acceptance of Mexican citizenship, clung to their native institutions such as African slavery. Determining that the tide needed to be stopped, he made a number of recommendations to the central government. Lucas Alaman, President Anastasio Bustamente's secretary of foreign relations, agreed that some brake was required to stop the continuing invasion of North Americans if Texas was to be saved for Mexico. The result was the celebrated Law of April 6, 1830, which was a marked reversal from previous Mexican policy with regard to Texas.

The law embodied a number of different provisions, but the most serious was to halt American immigration. By placing a positive interpretation on its negative statement, Austin and the other empresarios who were already legally operating assumed that they were exempt, at least as far as their present lands were concerned. But few Americans in Texas could easily accept the provision for the military occupation of the area, particularly since it specified that it be done with convict-soldiers. Equally repugnant was the authorization of customs collection posts in Texas. Those who had arrived earliest had been enjoying exemption from tariff duties for seven years, and even the tonnage dues on foreign vessels had gone largely uncollected—a kind of salutary neglect that had come to be expected by the Texans. But the exemption period was to expire in November, 1830, and now the immigrants were hit with another blow—no growth and new taxes. Austin tried to keep the Texans' reaction mild, and in fact there was little said until the manner of enforcement was known.

Teran's resources were ostensibly good. He was authorized to use $500,000 to perform his new duties, and he had 1,300 troops at his disposal for deployment in Texas. These were stationed at Nacogdoches, Bexar, and Goliad, where there were other troops already in residence; and new posts were created at Fort Teran, Velasco, and Anahuac. A customs collection house was also erected at Galveston for the purpose of enforcing the revenue collection provisions when they became operable. Teran's selection of personnel for commanding many of these posts was good. Don Domingo Ugartechea at Velasco, and even Jose de las Piedras at Nacogdoches, seem to have had a firm grasp on their commands if not the deep affection of the settlers in their respective regions. But the two men who represented Teran on Galveston Bay, George Fisher, the customs collector, and Colonel John David Bradburn, the military commander at Anahuac, were both bad choices.

Bradburn was the first to cause difficulty. A native of Kentucky, he had left the United States for Mexico in 1817 following a jailbreak. He and his brother, merchants in Springfield, Tennessee, had been detained in Columbia, Tennessee following a dispute over slave property, and they made their escape by sawing through the jail bars. His brother subsequently drowned, but John Davis Bradburn travelled down the river to New Orleans and made his way to Mexico in 1817. After the nationalist revolution, he joined the army as an officer and by 1830 he was in Matamoros, having risen to the rank of colonel. Teran conceivably selected him for the Anahuac post because he was an American, and he may have hoped that this would assist Bradburn in dealing with his own kind. Unfortunately, it only rendered him less suited for the position.[13] His personality was such that it clashed with his fellow countrymen, who, it is possible, may have expected too much favoritism from him.

The tinder box situation was clearly understood by Teran. He carefully instructed Bradburn to locate outside the limits of any established empresario's lands, to make a concerted effort to establish friendly relations with the settlers, and to show them that his presence meant protection for themselves and their property and a convenient marketplace for their produce. In the building of his quarters he was to employ local labor from the nearby settlement at Atascosito. It would be his job to settle families already there but to admit no more and specifically to admit no more slaves. And most importantly, his men were to be strictly disciplined and kept free of entanglements with the settlers. If most of these instructions had been followed, little trouble would have been caused. Unfortunately, most were violated.[14]

The American settlers already in the region were theoretically secure in their claims for land. The law of April 6, 1830, seemed to permit the continued granting of land to settlers on existing empresarial grants, and all of these still had available lands. There were hundreds of settlers already there, some of whom had a good many months, even years, invested in their lands, but because of the lack of opportunity or of inclination, they had never received legal titles. More importantly, hundreds more were already on their way to Texas as a result of the recruiting activities of the Galveston Bay and Texas Land Company, which operated on the assigned lands of David G. Burnet, Joseph Vehlein, and Lorenzo de Zavala. Their subsidiary, the Union Land Company, brought in 120 families after Bradburn had arrived and announced the suspension of land grants. Their plight was similar to that of the hundreds of others already there and to those who were arriving daily by land and by sea; together they suspected bad faith from everybody concerned.[15] In short, Anahuac was a powder keg.

The internal dispute among Mexican authorities now came into play. The government of Coahuila-Texas, prior to the passage of the Law of April 6, 1830, had appointed Juan Antonio Padilla as general land commissioner for the Department of Texas. He arrived in the eastern part of the state in February, 1830, intending to issue titles to the settlers there, but before he could begin his labors he was arrested for embezzlement and murder. To ease the fear that this was a ruse to keep their titles from the settlers, Padilla was hastily replaced by J. Francisco Madero. Before Madero could arrive, however, Bradburn had left Matamoros on November 17, 1830, with Lieutenant Juan Maria Pacho, his paymaster and customs man, Jose Rincon, his second in command, two additional officers and twenty-one men from the Twelfth Permanent Battalion, and nineteen other soldiers from various commands. He was to be joined later by other support from La Bahia. Bradburn arrived in Anahuac ahead of Madero, who reached San Felipe by mid-January, 1831, and the stage was set for a confrontation between these two frontier representatives of federalism and centralism, with the titleless settlers caught in the middle.

When Madero published his mission, Bradburn notified him that the issuance of titles would be in violation of the Law of April 6, 1830. Madero's response was that he did not intend to issue titles to the settlers who had arrived after the passage of the law, but his mission, under state authority, was to service those who had arrived earlier. Bradburn sought Teran's advice, but ordered Madero to desist; then on February 13, he arrested Madero and his surveyor, Jose Maria Carbajal.[16] Bradburn was quick to use his power to arrest, as many of the American settlers in Anahuac were to learn. Teran, although still at odds with the state authorities over his powers, soon ordered the release of Madero, and Madero started for San Antonio. Before he left, however, he established an *ayuntamiento* at Atascosito, and renamed it *Villa de la Satisima Trinidad de la Libertad*, or Liberty, as Americans called it. When Bradburn learned of this, he immediately suspended its operations and ordered an *ayuntamiento* for Anahuac. Again, this is evidence of a jurisdictional dispute between centralist and federalist authorities, but the American settlers were in the middle, and it looked to them as if local government, under their local control, was being usurped by a central-military figure. This would become a substantial grievance in the months ahead.

Meanwhile, Teran's other non-Mexican appointee, George Fisher, was provoking resentment elsewhere. Fisher was from Belgrade, which is in the province of Servia in the Ottoman Empire. He emigrated first to Germany, and then in 1815 came to Philadelphia, where he became an American citizen. He travelled to Mexico during its revolution from Spain, and again changed citizenship.[17] Teran selected Fisher for the position of customs collector on the Texas coast and in May, 1830, he arrived at San Felipe de Austin where he published his mission. He established his post at the mouth of the Brazos and sent a deputy to Galveston.[18] The first few months were uneventful as he busied himself with preparations to begin active customs collection when the seven-year exemption expired in November. Suddenly Teran suspended Fisher's position on the grounds that the Law of April 6, 1830 did not prohibit foreign vessels and therefore the collection of customs would be unnecessary. Fisher temporarily became secretary to the *ayuntamiento* at San Felipe de Austin; he was later suspended for disloyalty. He then returned to Matamoros, where he found various employment until September, 1831, when he was again given the customs post at Galveston, with Francisco Masue y Declor as his second in command.

Even as Teran had tried to help Bradburn grasp the nature of the situation in Texas, he futilely cautioned Fisher not to arouse the colonists. He even accompanied him to Galveston to establish the post. Teran, through letters to Austin and by other means of communication, also tried to allay the fears of the Americans. He seemed to draw clearly enough the lines of local authority and charged Fisher only with the collection of customs. As soon as he left, however, Fisher provoked the local citizens. On November 24, Fisher ordered that all ships intending to ply the Brazos had to first go to Anahuac for clearance; all merchants had to post a bond on their wares there also. This would work a considerable hardship on the coastal trade because it would require the vessels to sail past Galveston to the far end of the bay and then back out again. Also the shallowness of the mouth of the Trinity presented a navigational difficulty. Overland communication between the rivers was also a complicating factor. At the time of the order several American ships, the *Nelson,* the *Williams,* the *Ticson* and the *Sabine* were all in the Brazos. Edwin Waller, the owner of one of the ships, worked to persuade the commander at the mouth of the river not to enforce the order, and at Anahuac several merchants and other citizens tried in vain to secure recall of the order. Failing in his effort, Waller returned to his boat and ordered it to run past the troops. The *Sabine,* laden with cotton piled on the deck as protection, successfully made its escape, and the other vessels began to follow. Spencer Jack fired and wounded one of the Mexican soldiers as the *Sabine* passed the fort.[19] News of this incident and of the general unhappiness in Texas was naturally upsetting to Teran[20], but it was especially upsetting to the Texans also. To them the mere presence of a central government customs agent was threatening and his methods were abhorrent. Furthermore, Fisher and Bradburn vied with each other for power in Anahuac until Teran recalled Fisher in April, 1831. The colonists continued to be offended by the continuation of the customs order. Meetings were held in Brazoria, and a delegation led by Branch T. Archer called at Anahuac to protest its continuance.

Another, more grating irritation between the government and the colonists was caused by the personality of Bradburn and the conduct of the soldiers under his command. Under the best of circumstances soldiers who are far from home are often involved in activities that are resented by local residents. At Anahuac the soldiers were often without pay; and, although their barracks were as comfortable as most dwelling places in frontier Texas, the soldiers lacked the stabilizing forces that were demanded by the tense situation. Compounding their very presence, which was bad enough since they were regarded as "foreign" invaders in the same way Bostonians resented the redcoats in the 1770s, was their personal backgrounds. Although all were not convicts, this stigma was attached to them, and little time was lost in the erection of communications barriers between the settlers and the enlisted soldiers. Officers, the Mexican ones at least, had better relationships with the Americans, but the ranks were regarded as something less than civilized.

The settlers were soon buzzing with stories such as that of the drunken lieutenant, who, in celebration of his birthday, cursed the "Americanos" in Anahuac, and the ensuing excitement caused them to stand on the alert most of the night for fear that the soldiers would take up his cause.[21] There are many other accusations against the soldiers, including physical abuse, such as whipping a boy who could not carry an assigned load from a ship,[22] to molestation of a settler's wife by a wood cutting party,[23] to arbitrary and possibly unjustified arrest of the settlers who took matters into their own hands to punish the soldiers who did these things.

A showdown was clearly developing by the spring of 1832. The Texas settlers, many of them feeling deceived by the land companies or the government or both, grew increasingly angry over what was considered unjust treatment from Bradburn and Fisher, and these agents, particularly Bradburn, grew increasingly impatient with the settlers' disloyalty. It seems obvious that it was the agents, rather than the government, who were causing the trouble; but in any case, with all these forces involved, only a minor act would be required to precipitate a significant protest, even a revolt, although what the consequence or even its aim would be was not clear. Just when the settlers determined to resist Bradburn with force is difficult to determine. As early as December, 1831, or January, 1832,

Branch T. Archer and George B. McKinstry came from Brazoria to protest the order requiring all ships to call at Anahuac before plying the inland waters. Although ultimately successful, they apparently did not feel that Bradburn had acted in good faith. McKinstry wrote, "Before leaving Anahuac Archer and McKinstry entered into a *secret* understanding with Travis and some others to resist to the utmost the unlawful proceedings of the military and Custom House Officers . . . ." They then sent to New Orleans for powder, lead, and flint to enforce their arguments should force be necessary.[24] To conceal their purposes, the men of Anahuac organized themselves into a militia company for the avowed purpose of Indian defense, and elected Patrick C. Jack as their captain.

Just what were the grievances of the militia company and the others they represented? More immediate than the threat of unwanted customs and the suspension of the granting of land titles was the personality of Bradburn himself and his arbitrary use of power. Far from a superior officer, and himself the chief reporter to his commander of all his activities, Bradburn broadly interpreted his instructions to suit his purposes. Specifically, the colonists resented his impressment of supplies for his garrison without paying for them; his refusal to give the newly arrived settlers their promised lands, even though he did provide garden spots for sustenance; his use of uncompensated slave and citizen labor for the construction of barracks and customs houses; his activities with regard to the slaves that the Americans feared would bring about their release from bondage; and most immediately, his arbitrary arrest of two citizens and a declaration of martial law. This last offense involved Patrick Jack and Travis, and was the event that ultimately cast the shadow of revolt across all of Anglo-Texas.

Jack was arrested twice, and Travis once, but their cases are related. Jack was first arrested for accepting the captaincy of the militia company whose real purpose was transparent. He was jailed on an American vessel lying in the harbor. Several attempts were made by colonial leaders to secure his release, but it was not until Robert Williamson threatened Bradburn with personal harm that Jack was permitted to come ashore. When he did, his company received him with mocked ceremony, presenting him with an old, rusted sword as a badge of his office. Bradburn was understandably upset at this. He was a man who seemed to get more upset when away from his antagonist than when in his presence.

Next came the arrest of Travis. There are several differing accounts as to the cause. One suggests that his remonstrance to Bradburn over a whipping administered to a minor caused it; another, that it was caused by an altercation with Mexican soldiers following their accused rape of an Anglo woman. The most probable account involves Travis as an attorney and is borne out by the eyewitness testimony of both Labadie and Scates, and in communications from Monroe Edwards and others who alerted the settlement at San Felipe. It claims that Bradburn arrested Travis for causing him to look ridiculous before the citizens of Anahuac, something that was sure to get back to Teran one way or another.

The story began sometime after Jack's release, but bad feelings had existed for some time because of Bradburn's previous interference with the normal pattern of slave ownership and property rights as understood by southerners of that era. Bradburn, in much of his slave-related activities, was implementing government policy, but this was misunderstood by the colonists, most of whom either owned slaves or approved of the institution. The saga began when two or three slaves, the alleged property of William M. Logan of Opelousas, Louisiana, arrived in Anahuac and were harbored by Bradburn. When Logan arrived to claim them, he was told by Bradburn that he would have to secure papers proving ownership from the government in Louisiana before they could be released. Logan, before he left to obtain the necessary documents, engaged Travis as a local attorney to assist in claiming his property. When Logan returned with his legal documents, Bradburn asked for a day to consider them. When Logan returned for the second time he was told that the slaves had joined the Mexican army; they were therefore under the army's protection and could not be returned to Louisiana. Enter the local attorney. Amid general concern in Anahuac, rumors quickly reached Bradburn that armed help was coming from Louisiana to recapture Logan's slaves. This kind of intelligence was naturally unnerving to Bradburn, and when a letter warning of a hundred armed men already at the Sabine reached him he called out the garrison in the middle of the night and sent out scouts to locate the invaders. The populace of Anahuac was not officially informed as to the reason for this activity, but it is likely that they knew. A week passed, and the scouts returned with the information that no invaders could be found. Bradburn then began an inquiry into the integrity of the warning, and learned that the letter had been presented to the sentry on a dark night by a tall stranger who called him "Amigo," identified himself as Billew, and disappeared. Bradburn immediately suspected Travis, who was sometimes called Bill, and ordered him arrested. The soldiers found Travis in the office he shared with Jack; thus when the latter went along he soon found himself again under arrest. They were housed in the guard house, but Bradburn hurried the completion of two brick kilns which would become their jail. They were carefully watched, and letters they attempted to pass to friends were intercepted. Bradburn later claimed that these letters were to be sent to San Felipe to call for help, and were evidence of an impending revolt of the American colonials from Mexico. Hannah, a slave girl belonging to James Morgan, called daily with food and laundry, and the prisoners also received some internal assistance from Juan Cortina, Bradburn's second in command. But it was Hannah who carried out the mail, and when the authorities intercepted a letter addressed to "O.P.Q.," probably intended for Monroe Edwards, asking for a horse to be kept in readiness, Bradburn determined to move his prisoners to the more secure quarters.

The citizens of Anahuac tried from the first to secure the release of the prisoners. Colonel Morgan called on the first day they were arrested and pledged his entire property as bail. Others rode to inform Jack's brother, William, who arrived and remonstrated with Bradburn so vehemently that he was himself threatened with arrest. As the word spread across Anglo-Texas, the more hot-headed began to organize protest meetings at Brazoria and San Felipe, and from these gatherings armed men moved toward Liberty. Several of the meetings, however, were characterized by a wait-and-see spirit that usually produced pledges of loyalty to the government, indicating that the Americans were not united; but Bradburn was sufficiently alarmed to send his own riders to Velasco and Nacogdoches, seeking additional troops.

In Anahuac, Travis and Jack were moved to the kilns which Bradburn had constructed. Named "Morelos" and "Hidalgo," they were well fortified with a cannon. The garrison turned out to participate in the transfer; Labadie stood on his fence, tears in his eyes, to witness the procession. He called to Travis to be of good cheer, and Travis returned his greeting with a bow. Meanwhile, letters were furiously flying about the countryside. Teran demanded an investigation and called on Austin to use his influence to hold down the revolt. Ramon Musquiz, the political chief in San Antonio, did the same. As yet no formal charges were filed, and the future of the revolt hinged on how and where Travis and Jack would be tried. Bradburn announced a military trial, and Pacho busied himself with the process. A military trial for civilians was naturally resented, and this was intensified by his further announcement that they were to be moved to Matamoros for the actual proceedings. Although still not united, more Americans were incensed at this news, and a group hastened to the area of activity who were determined to free the prisoners by force if necessary. Seeking information, Bradburn sent out a patrol which was captured by the arriving Americans. Now with their own hostages, Francis W. Johnson, the elected leader, and Wyly Martin, William

Jack, Hugh Johnson and John Austin called on Bradburn. They claimed a peaceful mission—the securing of the prisoner's release—but they showed force. The affair then took an unexpected turn. Bradburn startled the delegation with the news that one of the company on his side of the table, Col. Felix Surbaran, was the new commander of the post. Surbaran had recently arrived from the interior of Mexico to secure the loyalty of Texas for General Antonio Lopez de Santa Anna, who was pressing a revolution and promising liberalization. The petitioners took Bradburn's announcement as a trick and threatened to attack. Bradburn ordered Jack and Travis staked to the ground and he stationed riflemen around them, promising their instant death at the first shot from the colonists. Travis begged the Americans to disregard his personal safety, but they left with only a threat against Bradburn should harm come to Travis and Jack. Two days later they met again at Bradburn's invitation, with Surbaran providing the intermediacy, and discussed an exchange of prisoners. The Americans agreed to release their Mexican prisoners and to receive Travis and Jack some twenty hours later. Many in the main camp, now grown to 160 men, were upset at this decision, but they agreed to wait and see what would happen. Their fears were confirmed when Bradburn not only refused to release Travis and Jack but also opened fire on the town, sending women and children scurrying for safety. Back at their camp, the Americans now took steps to formalize their organization. They adopted a series of platforms known as the Turtle Bayou Resolutions which declared their loyalty to Santa Anna, and they drew up a list of grievances against Bradburn. This news was received by the higher Mexican officials as confirmation of Bradburn's claim that the Americans had planned revolution all along. John Austin then took some of the men to Brazoria to secure two cannons left there by a ship that needed to be lightened to cross over a bar, and the men at Turtle Bayou awaited the artillery. It did not arrive in time, however; but in getting it past Ugartechea at Velasco, the first real blood of the summer was shed. Both sides sustained several dead and wounded. The shock of this bloodshed would ultimately cause both sides to review their purposes in Texas.

Back in Anahuac, the situation changed completely with the arrival of Jose de las Piedras from Nacogdoches. Piedras had orders to stop the disturbance any way he could, and he wisely took the most peaceful course. He held a conference with the Americans and learned their side of the argument before going into Anahuac. His correspondence reveals that the good faith he pledged to them masked his true feelings of resentment, but he did proceed to settle the issue, even at the expense of punishing the Mexican troops, who, perhaps ignorantly, later violated his truce by attempting to arrest some of the American representatives during the night. When he reached Anahuac Piedras held a conference with Bradburn and persuaded him to release the prisoners for a civil trial at Liberty. He also agreed to reimburse the Americans for claims against confiscated and damaged property. On July 3, Travis and Jack were released to Hugh Johnson and transported to Liberty for trial, but the trial was never held. Piedras' greatest contribution to easing the situation, however, was in relieving Bradburn of command. Bradburn was given the privilege of requesting his replacement, and Juan Cortina was put in charge. In his report to Teran, Piedras lay the whole misunderstanding to a convict-trustee named Ugarte who served Bradburn as a clerk and whom he charged with misrepresenting Bradburn in correspondence and misinforming him about the general situation. Bradburn hid out for a few days before escaping the wrath of the Americans, and especially the suspected vengeance of Travis, by fleeing on a horse, swimming the Sabine, and finally making his way to New Orleans before returning to Matamoras.

Musquiz was delighted to learn that the disturbance in his province was over, but Teran, despondent over his command and fearful of Santa Anna's success, fell on his own sword. The various American settlements, except at Nacogdoches, made their peace with Musquiz by pledging their loyalty. Piedras faced another crisis when he returned home, which culminated in the Battle of Nacog-doches.[25]

For Travis and Jack the events of April, June, and early July, 1832 were most propitious. Both, especially Travis in the light of later events, had been pushed to the fore-ground of those who were suspected by the Mexicans of favoring revolution and alignment with the United States. Many of the Americans, sobered by the return of peace, also held them in some suspicion as trouble makers. But for those who did already see or desire such revolution, they were also marked men, men who could be enlisted when the trouble came again. Nevertheless, most in Texas were content to watch the movements in central Mexico and hope for the return of federalism.

In Anahuac the troubles produced business stagnation, and many moved on to find work, or fortune, or more trouble. To Travis, it was a time for moving again. Anahuac had been but a brief interlude, a place where he had learned the Spanish language better but gained a con-tempt for Mexican ways and laws. He had no home, no wife, no ties to the coast with its memories of makeshift jails, mosquitos, and unhappiness. San Felipe now offered more of what he came to Texas to find—forgetfulness of Alabama and Rosanna, and making a name and a fortune. Once more he was on a horse, and after crossing another river, this time the Trinity, he was still moving west.

Actor Richard Carlson as Travis in The Last Command. *Carlson's performance drew heavily from the Travis personality interpreted by historian Amelia Williams.*
— Courtesy Republic Pictures, Forest View Historical Services

4

San Felipe

By now moving was not a new thing to William Barret
Travis. Only twenty-three years of age, he had moved
many times in his life, first as a boy from South Carolina
to Conecuh County, Alabama, from his father's farm to
Claiborne, and then the big move two years earlier to
Texas. Now he was moving again from Anahuac to the
political center of Anglo-Texas at San Felipe. San Felipe
was Stephen F. Austin's headquarters, the principal place
that new settlers went to get land assignments, and a likely
location for developing a legal trade. Travis, who was
now very much involved in politics and interested in making a fortune, could not miss its strategic value. And he
moved around anyway. Separated from his wife and tied
to no particular place, he easily acquired the habit of
hanging his hat at the end of a day's travel and considering
wherever he was as home. This was necessary for a frontier lawyer; he had to go to the business. But the impression is inescapable that Travis simply liked to travel, to
meet people and firm up contacts—perhaps against some
future use—and to see new country. He was the kind of
man who might romanticize the destinations that would
be reached along the dusty Texas roads, yet he was practical and calculating, and he shrewdly took advantage of
business opportunities along the way.

It is easy to see him riding into San Felipe. His route from Anahuac probably had been an indirect one, punctuated by little visitations along the way. He was, after all, an object of considerable attention in that summer of 1832, having been a sufferer in Bradburn's makeshift prison. Young enough for most women to mother, and old enough to make the others react in different ways, he was apparently a welcomed guest. There were rivers and creeks to ford, and many prairie miles to cross on the way to San Felipe. The town was well developed by the summer of 1832. It was still the headquarters of Austin's colony, but the empresario himself seemed always to be away on the colony's business. It was the seat of the *ayuntamiento*, and sooner or later all important people and affairs came through or ended up there. There were several stores, some boarding houses, a tavern, and several cabins. Travis was already known at Peyton's where he had often gone with Robert Williamson, and he stayed there first. In the years he lived in San Felipe he lived at many places, however, and he hung his shingle on even more. He lived for a while, for instance, in a house owned by John Rice Jones. He officed at a place called the White House which he rented from Silas Dinsmore, but then he moved his business to a house owned by Dr. James B. Miller. The latter facility also offered a stable. The horse, being the omni-present element in all transportation, was essential, and Travis owned several. In a diary kept during part of his stay in San Felipe, he mentioned a black, a dun, a bay, and a Spanish pony as being his.[1] Like many others he engaged in the active buying and selling of such livestock, and he seems to have had several stabled in various places against future need. When stopping to visit at a cabin he sometimes lost his horse and had to walk home, and on at least one occasion was thrown from his horse. It seems likely that Travis used horses rather than worshipped them, and that he may have even been a little careless with them.

When Travis began his residence in San Felipe at Peyton's, the hostelry, was operated by Jonathan C. Peyton and his wife. It was a real home, and the Peyton's daughter, "Mag" must have reminded him of his own chilren in Alabama. She was the pet of the household, and Travis, like the others, patronized her with small presents, including a pair of shoes. His own youthfulness is revealed in a prank he and Williamson played on Mrs. Peyton. She ran a two-table boarding house. The rougher, staple type food was placed on the table for the men, but more tasty items found their way to her own table, which was also used by the ladies. Williamson diverted the ladies' attention by regaling them with flattery while Travis and the others exchanged the provisions of the two tables, and then the men enjoyed the finer fare.[2] Such pranks may have occasionally rendered him *personna non grata* at Mrs. Peyton's table, or he may have just wanted a change, but he also dined elsewhere during his stay in San Felipe, including the boarding table of Mrs. Jane Wilkins, at Gay and Adam's, and when he was in Brazoria, at Mrs. Longs. In September, 1833 he thought seriously of moving to Brazoria after receiving an offer of office space, along with the promise of plenty of business there, but he decided to stay on in San Felipe.

Travis' education did not make him unique on the Texas frontier, but it was above average and he strove to keep it so. He also supported the education of the young. Often he made arrangements for the children of his acquaintances to be tutored, and he was cited by some schoolmasters as a reference when seeking employment, an indication that he kept up with educational practices. His will specified that his children were to receive a good education—Charles Edward through the college level, and Susan Isabella an "ample and complete English Education."[3] But he did not neglect his own mind, and he was known as a dedicated reader. He often borrowed books in the way that such treasured items must be shared on the frontier to preserve the seeds of civilization, and he seems to have been good about returning them, a condition, no doubt, of borrowing more as well as a testimony of his own character. Whatever else he may have lacked in

85

morality, he was above reproach when dealing with the property of others. Among the works that Travis read were Herodotus' *History*, and an anonymous work, *Court and Camp of Bonaparte*, first published in 1831 and later republished in 1837 as part of the Harper Family Library. He also read P. C. Headley's *Life of Empress Josephine*, several works by Febrero, and a "Bolinbroke Study of History," probably his *Letters on the Study and Use of History*, published in London in 1752. He also read *Yankee Among the Nullifers*, by A. Green, Eliza Leslie's *Pencil Sketches, or Outlines of Character and Manners*, and an almanac. In fiction he liked historical novels. He read James K. Paulding's *The Dutchman's Fireside* and a romance entitled *Westward Ho!* He also read Jane Porter's *Scottish Chiefs*, Catherine Maria Sedgwick's *Hope Leslie*, and John Richardson's *Wacousta*. Among the English or Scottish writers he read were Disraeli's *Vivian Grey*, Tobias Smollett's *The Adventures of Ferdinand, Count Fathom*, and *Rob Roy*. This list, which was compiled from his diary references, probably represents only a sample of his reading while in Texas but it is testimony to the available materials.[4] He also did a little writing. In addition to a diary, he kept a work docket to record his legal business, and shortly after coming to San Felipe he wrote an autobiography which is not extant. And Travis was willing to share his professional knowledge. In May, 1834, he made a bargain with J. Hampton Kuykendall to work in the office as an apprentice. His labors as an office boy and copier were obviously needed by Travis, but the education which young Kuykendall was to receive should have amply repaid him.

In life-style Travis lived much as a young man on the frontier would be expected to live. His diversions were dictated by availability and opportunity, and were often lusty. He gambled, for instance, but did not expect to become wealthy from the games he played, which included poker, three-card monte, and ecucre, a game played with the higher cards of each suit. He evidently gambled to pass the time, to be sociable, to gain business contacts or for similar motives. Most of his losses or gains were relatively minor after several hours of play, but occasionally they would run as high as thirty or forty dollars. Travis bet on the outcome of Robert Williamson's election as alcalde of San Felipe, and won himself a new ten dollar hat. Another political bet netted him a new pair of boots. His sagacity at predicting the outcome of political contests seems to have been better than his luck with cards, but it was perhaps his own campaigning efforts in Williamson's behalf that hedged his bet.

Travis was not a heavy drinker, but he did occasionally visit John Barleycorn. He sometimes recorded in his diary the purchase of whiskey and glasses for its consumption, probably intended as a gift that was to be shared with the donor. Perhaps it was drunkenness among the male guests at the holiday ball in December, 1833 that provoked his reference to "Hell among the women about party." He did very much enjoy going to parties and balls. He often paid subscriptions to attend them, and once suggested a dance to celebrate the conclusion of a legal matter, but his hostess diverted the activity to a preaching and hymn-singing fest. The common image of Travis is that of a dandy, and in this the legend may not be far from the truth. He dressed well and was conscious of personal appearance. He bought boots, gloves, and hats, all of which were necessities to his time and place, but he seems to have changed them with stylish regularity, and he often purchased material for the making of shirts. He hired these made by a variety of people, and he was not above returning something that did not fit properly. He once remarked in his diary how well something made him look, and in an age when many men did not bother with the wearing of stockings, or socks, he bought them by the half-dozen. He also hired his washing done regularly. Again, there is a practical side to this: he was in the public eye, he represented people at court, and he became a government official. But his concern with clothes is beyond the norm, and he could be called fastidious, if not vain.

Travis remained something of an outdoorsman. He apparently did not hunt, but he frequently went fishing, particularly in the company of young ladies, which may have been an excuse to be alone with them. But he apparently really did fish, at least enough to provide a meal.

Travis was unquestionably a charitable and generous man. A thoughtful guest, he often brought presents to his hostesses or sent them little mementos after his visit. He frequently gave large gratuities to those who did him minor favors, such as holding his horse. Sometimes these gifts were spontaneous, especially to children, and one imagines that he could not help thinking of his own at such times. He once bought five dollars worth of "goods" for charity distribution; he allowed many people to sleep over night in his office; and he was apparently an easy touch for a hard luck story. He also borrowed and lent money in the same day, for the same amount, indicating that the purpose all along had been to convenience someone else. But he paid his debts, and expected the same courtesy in return. When repayment was not forthcoming he could be unyielding, as when he had an F. Robidoux "siezed" for failing to pay a debt in 1833. And although his professional fortunes improved, he remained conscious of the value of money, feeling that a haberdashery charge of two dollars and fifty cents was "exorbitant." Travis' upbringing or the frontier need for human dependence often found outlet in his willingness to sit up at night with people who were ill, or to help with funeral arrangements when that was necessary.

The depth of his religious conviction is difficult to determine. His relations with Alexander Travis would have grounded him firmly in the tenents of Christianity, particularly of the Baptist beliefs. Frontier Texas did not afford much opportunity for pious public worship. He did attend preachings, and apparently liked the company of Godly-men as well as the worldly. He made financial gifts to several men of the cloth, and a Padre Jean used his office for a room and ate for a while at a San Felipe boarding table at his expense. The greatest claim Travis has to religiousity, however, involves a letter he wrote in August, 1835 to the *New York Christian Advocate and Journal.* The purpose of the communication was to subscribe to the publication, but he claimed double duty from his postage by requesting that some religious work be begun in Texas. "We are very destitute of religious instruction in this extensive fine country, and the circulation of your paper here will be greatly beneficial in the absence of the stated preaching of the Gospel." He indicated that religious practices were no longer expressly forbidden, but that few clerics had come to Texas". . . . to dispense the tidings of salvation to upwards of sixty thousands of destitute souls." He lamented the overlooking of Texas by the Methodist itinerancy, and requested that the editor publish his letter to inform the Bishops of the different Conferences as well as the Board of Missions of the need of preachers in Texas. "About five educated and talented young preachers would find employment . . .", he promised, and concluded with the plea "In sending your heralds to the four corners of the earth, remember Texas."[5] There is no reason to doubt the sincerity of Travis' appeal, which reveals a good knowledge of the Methodist Church structure. Still his own convictions are not clear. Probably he was content to rest on the teaching of Uncle Alex and had little doubt about his own salvation, despite his present life-style as a back slider. Travis' life in Texas often did not reflect those teachings in regard to the Seventh Commandment.

At least once Travis was willing to back up the right of worship with force, although his motives may have been as much political as religious. In 1834, the Reverend John Wesley Kenny came to Washington-on-the-Brazos and held a service, then moved on to Holly Springs for a camp meeting. The prospects were good for further religious work, and he wanted to return the following year. There was concern that the troubled situation would cause some difficulty with the government, but the community leaders, including Travis, encouraged the preacher to go ahead with his plans and pledged their presence and support that his meetings would not be troubled.[6]

Travis' professional activities grew with his continued residence in San Felipe. The partnership with Patrick Jack was apparently not continued after he left Anahuac, but his business did not suffer with a single practice. He practiced alone for most of the remainder of his professional life, although the press of business did make him occasionally think of taking a partner. In 1835 he worked out such an arrangement with Thomas Willis Nibbs, and he also briefly partnered with Franklin J. Starr. Travis' lost legal docket might have offered great insight regarding his career at this time, but there is enough correspondence to indicate the nature of his business activities. Among the earliest evidence of his legal business in San Felipe is a letter to O. H. Allen of Brazoria asking Allen to appear before the court there in behalf of Mr. DeCrow. He reminded Allen that the case would turn ". . . on the question of whether the sea & its shores are the common property of all mankind . . . ," but would make no further suggestions ". . . to one so capable of managing the cause to advantage . . . ," but he cautioned, "I am told that in Mr. Wightman we have a Wiley adversary."[7] He was employed frequently in probate cases, land transactions, bills of sale, and in the drawing of wills.[8] The pay was often in kind, or at least in some form of note. Frequently he was engaged to collect notes for others. James F. Perry thus engaged him to collect unpaid notes on Gabriel Cole, E. Roddy, Thomas Slaughter, James Ross, and others in June, 1835; he was to receive five percent of the amount collected for his services. He also enjoyed the business of many prominent Texas developers and businessmen. For instance, in 1834 and 1835 he was the attorney for Robert Wilson and David Harris and the Harris estate, and was also among the subscribers of land to support their venture to introduce service by sea from New Orleans.[9] Travis was also an occasional litigant. In June, 1834, he was engaged in a suit against a man named Galleher, and was himself sued by R. J. Mosely. He also mentions being "dunned" for a debt by P. C. Jack, but apparently this disagreement did not make it to court.[10]

A glimpse of Travis as a trial lawyer at work is provided by Mrs. Dilue Harris. In April, 1834, Dr. Pleasant W. Rose played host to a court meeting to settle a disagreement between two of his neighbors, called Mr. "A" and Mr. "M" in his daughter's reminiscences. Bad blood had existed between the two for some time, and this case only helped to increase it; indeed, "M" was stabbed to death at a later date. The dispute resulted from "A's" accusation that "M" had stolen his unbranded calf and affixed his own mark. The court that assembled to hear the case, and incidently brought excitement to the Rose household, was composed of David G. Burnet, John W. Moore and others, and the lawyers present included Travis, Patrick and William Jack, and Williamson. Families came from miles around to see the show, the men to watch and visit, and the women to cook and to take advantage of the female companionship. Ben Fort Smith offered to barbeque two calves to help the party along. The Rose children, including Mrs. Harris, were delighted to have Travis as a dinner guest before the trial, and listened as he and their father talked land. Then they assumed the best seat at the trial, held under a live oak tree, which was their playhouse under the trees. The playhouse was also used as a sleeping area for the men, where each stored his saddle, gun, water gourd, and eating utensils, including a knife and tin cup. The trial started at eleven in the morning and proceeded rapidly. Despite the obviousness of "M's" guilt, proven by the calf with his brand sucking a cow with "A's" brand, a situation considered conclusive in cow country, there was some concern that a verdict of guilty would send "M" to a Mexican jail. Nevertheless, the jury pronounced him guilty. Travis gave quick notice of appeal and Burnet granted it. The court and its gathering then adjourned to the barbeque that had been prepared by Smith, and while they ate, Smith drew "A" aside and bought both cow and calf. As the new owner, Smith convinced the court that the branding must have been the result of a mistake, and as the new owner he requested that the charges against "M" be dropped. In a move dictated more by politics than justice, the court agreed.

Some of the younger men then proposed a dance, but Mrs. Rose, who claimed she had not been to a worship service since coming to Texas, requested Divine Supplication instead. Since Mrs. Rose's Bible had been lost none was available for Scripture reading, but a Mr. Woodruff offered up a prayer exhorting people to live better lives, perhaps with "M" in mind, and Mrs. Rose sang, "Come, Thou Fount of Every Blessing." Travis promised the Rose girls that he would send them some side combs to play with in their house, and that he would find a Bible for Mrs. Rose. Later he did send two little books to the girls, which were cherished until abandoned in the Runaway Scrape after Travis' death. But he had to report that San Felipe did not afford a Bible for sale.[11]

When he first came to Texas Travis labored under the disadvantage of being forced to do written legal work in a foreign tongue. By 1833, however, he was expert enough in the language to write a bill of sale and presumably other work in Spanish, although some of the official papers of the *ayuntamiento* of San Felipe was done by an interpreter after Travis joined that body in an official capacity. Still, by the end of 1834 he was among the first rank in Texas attorneys.

Travis' estate grew with the passing months, especially when measured in land. He waited until 1835 to claim his land rights as a colonist, but he steadily acquired property all along. As early as August 15, 1832, he acquired a quarter-league plot from Francis J. Haskins that was situated on the Buffalo Bayou. In a letter to Austin, Haskins identified the land as adjoining that on which William Vince resided, and noted that there was a house and other improvements on the land.[12] In 1833 Travis purchased another quarter league from the division of lands held by Brown and Belknap in present Fort Bend County, and in January of that same year he purchased one hundred acres from James Stuart, paying for the land with livestock which was valued at sixty-two dollars and fifty cents each. The tract contained twelve acres of cleared land, a house and garden, and was apparently located close to San Felipe. In the settlement of his estate John Rice Jones advertised several other blocks of land which belonged to Travis, some no doubt acquired as payment for legal work. He apparently had a sufficiency, because he offered to subsidize the Harris-Wilson sailing scheme with five hundred acres. In 1835 he finally got around to applying for his headright as a colonist. On Williamson's advice he selected land in the Benjamin Milam grant. Curiously, he listed himself as a widower, probably his euphemism for being separated; or perhaps he thought that Rosanna had divorced him, for he had agreed to such action by then.

Travis drew up a will in 1835, also testimony that some fundamental change had occurred in his life and that he had accrued sufficient property to need to order its disposition. Rosanna is left out completely, again signifying that he had cut all ties with her by this time. The will, in the hand of John Rice Jones, is preserved in the State Library at Austin. Following the customary qualifying jargon of such documents it divided his property equally between his children, perhaps his first recognition of Susan Isabella. And most curiously, he gave her a slight advantage by specifying that she should receive that portion of his inheritance that came from his father's estate. The children were identified as his sole heirs, and were to come into the property ". . . as soon as they became of age or marry." In the meantime, the property was to be in the charge of guardians. For Charles Edward, he appointed the Reverend James A. Butler of Alabama with the direction that Charles be given a good collegiate education. Should Butler fail to accept the responsibility, John Rice Jones was named as his alternate. For Susan, her uncle, William M. Cato, was selected as guardian, with Jones again as second choice. Henry Smith was appointed as executor of the will, but in the end, it was again Jones who discharged the responsibility. The will was signed without witnesses at San Felipe on May 25, 1835.

The conditions of the will, and its omission of Rosanna, can be understood from an examination of Travis' relations with women after coming to Texas, and particularly from his severing of all ties with his wife. Shortly after moving to San Felipe, he made an agreement with an H. Sewell to go to Alabama to get his "paper," undoubtedly an attempt to cancel all debts there. But the matter with Rosanna could not be terminated so easily. Indeed, he showed no haste in wanting to do so, partially because the miles between them did an effective job of insulating him from the need to do so, and he had no intention of living chastely anyway. He may have used the widower gimic for convenience, but he was not reluctant to indulge his physical appetites. His first liason in Texas may have been the washerwoman Malinda, for he mentions in his diary paying an "M" for such services. In one diary passage he confessed an amorous venture with a woman, which he calculated to be number fifty-six in his life. The number, in itself rather astounding, is overshadowed by the fact that he had bothered to count. Sometime later a Susanna is listed as number fifty-nine, with the missing two apparently not being worthy of mention. On another occasion he records making love with a "C", and giving her a dollar. All of his relations with the ladies were by no means this sordid. He also mentions sending presents to a Miss Henry, suggesting that he was pressing a more honorable suit, and in 1833 he met the real love he was to find in Texas. She was Rebeca Cummings, who lived at Mill Creek with her brother. Travis no doubt met her when attending her brother's legal business. His trips to Mill Creek became frequent in late 1833 and continued during 1834, and the diary references to his visits with Rebeca take on the air of a genuine love story. In February, 1834 he told her about Rosanna, and suggested that his proposals, presumably to continue to see her, were "agreeably recd." He often wrote to her from San Felipe when he could not get to Mill Creek. Once he started to see her but found ". . . waters all

94

swimming & prarie so boggy—could not go—the first time I ever turned back in my life—." When he could get through, he described their meeting as "Intrigue—Bargain & management—successful—Staid all night at Cummins." On this visit he gave Rebeca a breast pin and accepted a lock of her hair and a ring. Later in the month he was so anxious to get there to show her a letter from Rosanna, perhaps to prove his sincerity in working out his problem, that he borrowed a horse to make the journey. The horse ran away, stranding him at Mill Creek, but he did not seem to mind for he "Spent day pleasantly in *la sociedad de me inamorata—*." Travis cautiously recorded many of his affairs of the heart in Spanish. When Rebeca had heard of some indiscretion or did not think he was moving fast enough on the arrangements for his divorce his reception was not so cordial. Such times would usually end up like this: "reception cold—but conclusion very hot;" "Spent day at C's, Last night a simple misunderstanding;" or "Hell—L-v-e triumphed over slander &—staid all night at C's." Gradually they arrived at an understanding, and on April 20, 1834, he recorded "Arrangement to wait till divorce is effected—& then—to marry." After that the references to Rebeca were mostly felicitous, such as "Went to Mill Creek—joyously received;" "Staid at Cummins all night—*buena*;" and "staid all night at Cummins—reconciliation—happy &—."

Travis was apparently ill much of this time with, as he called it, "venerao malo." Three times he purchased a vial of medicine identified as mercury for the malady, but he seemed to have had some difficulty in recovering, and this may have delayed his remarriage. But the largest single stumbling block was the fact that he already had a wife.

While he apparently never entertained the thought of going back to Rosanna, he continued to communicate with her during 1833 and 1834, and occasionally sent money to her. He wrote to her brother a good deal and many of his letters to his father were concerned with his marriage problems. They finally began to discuss the possibility of divorce. In January, 1834, he received a letter from Rosanna in which she expressed a willingness to let him have Charles Edward. He requested that his son be sent to Brazoria to the care of a Mrs. Long, but some difficulty developed in this arrangement. He later asked Monroe Edwards to go to Alabama for Charles, but this plan also proved unfruitful. So in March, he engaged William P. Huff to go to New Orleans to get Charles, who was there with his mother. This last attempt was successful, and Charles came to live in Washington County with the family of David Ayers.

For Rosanna's side of the story the best single source of information is a letter she wrote to James Dellet in September, 1834, from Natchez, Mississippi engaging his help in securing a divorce. She claimed that she had been urged by her friends for some time to seek the divorce, but had only lately lost confidence that he would return for her. She stated that he had led her to believe that he would return by writing to her of his affection with repeated assurances of his unchanging attachment, but that time passed and no tangible evidence of his intention to return was manifest. Finally her brother wrote to Travis ". . . stating in plain language his suspicion . . ." that he intended to abandon her permanently, and ". . . demanded an explicit explanation of his conduct and future intentions. . . ." Travis, she continued, then acknowledged that he never would return and wished to be permanently separated from her. Rosanna told Dellet that ". . . after the declaration of such a wish on his part I could no longer oppose my friends however painful the thought may be to my feeling to be separated from the father of my children while he is living independent of the disgrace that may attach itself to him myself or my children . . . , but Sir I must submit to this mortification with nothing but the knowledge of my own inocence as to the causes that has led to this result. . . ." Rosanna clearly sought to place the full blame on Travis for the separation, for she stated that ". . . so far as I was able to do so, or know how I endeavored to perform my duty as a wife with the most undeviating integrity and faithfulness and if any thing oc-

curred to dissatisfy him with me it was the result of my ignorance as to what was my duty as a wife, or I would have
performed it to his entire satisfaction." She wanted the
matter settled as soon as possible, she claimed, and then
grew more bitter in her indictment of Travis. She came to
New Orleans in the winter of 1833-34 with the expectation
of seeing Travis and making an arrangement about
Charles, whom she evidently believed belonged with his
father regardless of their own situation, ". . . but he disappointed me, here too." Evidently Travis had sent Huff to
bring his son without going personally to meet her.[13]

With Rebeca on his mind Travis did not object to the
divorce, and in the autumn of 1835 the Marion County
court pronounced the divorce. The Alabama legislature
sanctioned the dissolution of the marriage on January 9
1836.[14] There are several legends that Rosanna came to
Texas in 1835 to make one last attempt to see Travis. One
holds that they met in San Felipe, one in Galveston, and
still another in San Augustine. In any case, the action was
probably more a legal requirement than a sincere attempt
at reconciliation at so late a date, and on February 14,
1836, Rosanna was remarried to Samuel G. Cloud at
Monroeville, Alabama. Cloud was a planter from Louisiana, near Natchez, Mississippi, and she may well have
been under his care and influence when she wrote to Dellet
in 1834. There is a strong possibility that Cloud was
related to Dellet's wife, for several items of correspondence indicating some relationship are in the Dellet
papers.

There is no way to know Travis' reaction to the news of
his divorce, if he ever heard about it. Certainly he knew
that the proceedings were underway for he and Rebeca
were planning for the day that he would be free to re-
marry. But his political involvement in late 1835 and 1836
probably kept him from ever learning that he was a free
man. Rebeca later married David Y. Portis on December
28, 1843 in Austin County, Texas. She and Travis may
have parted before his public services called him away,
however, for there is a legend in the Mill Creek country

that Rebeca once had a lover who, after some trouble with her brother, went away and did not return. The nature of the difficulty or the identity of the man is not a part of the legend. If his diary can be trusted, Travis' affection for Rebeca seemed genuine, and a man who disliked turning back as much as he did would hardly be deterred by such a trifle as an angry brother. After all, William Cato had not done much with him. It is likely that if they decided to part company the decision was solely between them. It is even more likely that if he had lived beyond the revolution that Rebeca, or at least some Texas woman, would have again brought him to the altar. He had a son to raise, an estate to enlarge, and apparently the ability to feel deeply for someone, at least for a while. But now he had a splendid fortune to seek which lay along the course of political activism. San Felipe was the perfect spot for such a course, and for a while he was staying put.

5

Politician

SAN FELIPE presented a considerable contrast from Anahuac. There were fewer trees and more open space; the air was dryer; and the mosquitoes were not as large. And the political climate, particularly for Travis, was at least for a while a little cooler. The town hummed with activity and there was a sufficiency of legal business to support him in high style, considering the frontier surroundings. While he amused himself with Rebeca, or read Scott, or pursued the diversions and pastimes that were available to him, other men pursued the consequences of the disturbances of 1832 and 1833. In time Travis would also be swept along in these consequences; indeed, he would become a major actor in them once more. For some months after he arrived in town, however, he remained aloof from most public affairs. Perhaps he was busy with his private or professional life; perhaps he was aware that not everyone in Texas approved of the kind of violence and trouble making with which he had been associated at Anahuac. Whatever the reason, Travis was not the sort to keep his light under a bushel for long. When he crossed the Alabama River to come to Texas all caution if not prudence left him. He was in Texas not so much to escape Rosanna and all that she meant as he was to make his mark in the world, to assemble a fortune, and to be remembered. There were many of Travis' kind in San Felipe, and it is probable that it took him a while to convince the others that he was worth a second look. Despite Travis' occasional protest to friends that he did not keep up with political affairs, it is a good bet that he was a close observer of the consequences of the earlier disturbances, for when the opportunity again presented itself he was ready to step in.

The earlier trouble in Anahuac and Velasco had produced the convention spirit in Texas. The appearance of Santa Anna as a states' righter, deceiving as it was, was encouraging to many Texans, and out of the convention which met at San Felipe in October, 1832 came the additional call for statehood separate from Coahuila. They also asked for the repeal of the Law of April 6, 1830, for the renewed right of importing commodities free of duty from the United States, and for the privilege of creating a standing central committee at San Felipe with satelite committees in other towns which could keep the colonists informed on matters of national and local importance. Whether or not these requests were accepted, particularly in regard to the committees, they contained the seeds of rebellion. The committees are similar to the Committees of Correspondence which operated in the American colonies in the 1770s.

Travis was not on the original committee, but it contained men like him who were anything but conservative in their attitudes toward the centralizing influences from the south. He became a member of the committee in October, 1832, joining James B. Miller, Robert Peebles, Francis W. Johnson, Wyly Martin, William Pettus, and William H. Jack. Austin was still the peace, or conciliation, leader, but his mission to Mexico would remove a powerful force for cooperation.

The conservative element was still in control in Bexar, and from that quarter came requests that the committee be abandoned and that its delegates, William H. Wharton and Rafael Manchola, not be sent to the central

100

government with the convention's requests. The more radical group in San Felipe hesitated but by November, 1832, they determined to call a second convention. Austin, who had listened to the Bexar recommendations, endorsed them and even made pledges of support for them. He was embarrassed by the call for the second convention, but he was powerless to stop it, and an election was held on March 1, 1833 for the selection of delegates to the new conclave. Over fifty delegates assembled in San Felipe on April 1 for what proved to be a thirteen day session. The assembly selected the more radical Wharton over Austin as president, re-adopted the resolution of 1832, and this time drafted a proposed constitution for Texas as a separate state. Then they selected Austin, Miller, and Erasmo Seguin to bear their incendiary requests to the central government, recognizing that Austin could probably accomplish more than anyone else at this level of negotiation. In the end Austin went alone to Mexico. Many months passed before he saw Texas again.

His trip was unpleasant and the stay in Mexico City unproductive. Even the patient Austin finally grew weary of the fluctuations in power and vacillations in personality that gave him pleasant but noncommital interviews, and, after extended negotiations, no results. In anger he wrote on October 2, 1834 to the *ayuntamiento* at San Antonio that it might as well be about the business of organizing a provisional state government. Without his knowing it, the San Antonians returned copies of his treasonous letter through channels to the government. Austin was left at liberty until he started home in December. When he arrived at Saltillo on January 3, 1834, he was arrested and returned to Mexico City for many months of imprisonment. The arrest of Austin coincided with a lessening of the statehood fever in Texas, where fears for his safety helped to cool even the most radical. When he again communicated with Texas, Austin urged peaceful relations with Mexico, not for his own but for the colonists' safety. But as the months passed, he began to wonder if his friends had forgotten him. They had not, but time was needed for men like Travis to reassert control.

Travis became politically active again in 1834 when he accepted a position as secretary to the *ayuntamiento* at San Felipe. Robert Williamson was the *alcalde,* and he and Travis had the administrative responsibility for putting into effect the orders and directives of the state and national governments, and for informing the government about conditions within their district. All of this had to be conducted in the official language, and Travis enjoyed the services of a clerk-translator. Travis was not a member of the *ayuntamiento* and therefore could not vote; but as its secretary he could speak and perhaps influence the vote of others. By whatever means, he had become a leader in the decisions and actions of the body by the end of his one year term.

Austin's imprisonment caused the *ayuntamiento* concern. Not wishing to further endanger him by rashness, they did their best to honor his request for quiet. They also began a campaign to shift responsibility for his mission to themselves. During April and May the councils at San Felipe, Matagorda, Liberty, Bastrop, Gonzales and Brazoria forwarded resolutions claiming responsibility for the convention and praying for Austin to be set free. They explained his actions as those of an able representative, not an individual pursuing his own opinions. San Felipe adopted their resolution on April 28. In addition to the more formal communication with the government the resolution was circulated as a broadside and published in newspapers, and it probably spurred the other councils into action. A copy of the handbill signed by Travis and Williamson was sent to the Political Chief at San Antonio, Ramon Musquiz. The authorship of the resolution in unknown. Travis and Williamson probably had something to do with it, but they may have merely signed it as administrative officers certifying its official status. These efforts in Austin's behalf were, as he had requested, orderly and in due process of governmental action. As the months passed, however, Austin began to wonder if they were doing anything at all in his behalf, so quiet did Texas appear. Peter Grayson and Spencer Jack learned of his despair and travelled to Mexico to help free him. They were armed with the resolutions plus recommendations from Mexican officials, and they were able to secure his release from prison. He was detained in Mexico for several additional months, and he did not reach Texas again until September, 1835, after more violence had occurred.

Travis had other political business at San Felipe during this time. In March, 1834, the legislature of Coahuila and Texas created a Department of Brazos, entitling it to a Political Chief, an administrative position higher than *alcalde*. The governor requested the *ayuntamiento* to recommend three nominees from which he would select the first chief, whose term would continue until a general election was held in May, 1835. Williamson, J. H. C. Miller, and Travis were nominated. Travis wrote to Ramon Musquiz, who would communicate the nominations, that he had ". . . no desire to be employed in the position of Chief; but if I were named I should comply with all the laws and orders of the government to the best of my ability."[1] He also informed Musquiz that Miller ". . . is neither a colonist nor a naturalized citizen by law. Therefore he has no eligibility for the said office." It is difficult to determine whether self-advancement or preventing Miller from getting the job is the motivation for this letter. He said nothing about Williamson, his old friend from Anahuac and now a close confederate at San Felipe. Governor Agustin Viesca disregarded the nominations anyway and appointed Henry Smith of Brazoria as the Political Chief. It is possible that he disarmed the position by naming a man who was not a resident of the designated seat of government for the Department, thus slowing the pace of Anglo cooperation; it is also possible that he did not want Williamson or Travis, who had shown their colors at

Anahuac. Travis bore Smith no resentment for getting the job, but he did complain often about the latter's absence from San Felipe and the added labor this caused him with correspondence and with work that was left undone. He cheerfully congratulated Smith on being ". . . the first American who has been appointed to the office of Political Chief . . ." and expressed the hope that he would be the means of great good to Texas.[2] He also pressed Smith to come to San Felipe because there was a large number of documents there addressed to him as Political Chief, ". . . the contents of which we are anxious to know. We hope you will soon be here to gratify the wishes of the citizens." He also informed Smith that his new job would provide him with an annual salary of $880 and a clerk.

Smith assumed his office amid continued political stress. The centralist versus states' rights controversy was still raging, emphasized by a struggle between Monclova and Saltillo, each of which vied for recognition as the capital of Coahuila and Texas. Saltillo was the traditional seat of government for the state, and it tried to take advantage of Monclova's association with forces hostile to Santa Anna by declaring for him. With this dispute going on in the competitive captials, many in Texas mistakenly assumed that the time was ripe for them to make a play for separation. Oliver Jones, who was present in Coahuila with Williamson, joined him in urging Smith to call a convention to strike for independent statehood. On October 4, Smith wrote to Travis for advice. First Travis urged Smith to come to San Felipe at once where his presence was required more than ever before. With false modesty he claimed that his opinion was worthless because he paid little attention to politics; then he launched into strong advice to the Political Chief. Travis told Smith that Texas would be forever ruined if the citizens did not make a manly, energetic effort to save themselves from anarchy and confusion, the worst of their enemies. To avoid this, he urged, the central committee should call a constitutional

104

assembly to meet at either San Felipe or Bexar. Travis based the committee's authority to do so on the powers already vested on it, on the *ayuntamientos*, and on the Political Chief, and above all, on the necessity of circumstance, ". . . for, we are virtually an *ipso facto* without any legal government in the state or nation." Because of the developments in Coahuila, he reasoned, the Texans were no longer legally or constitutionally subject to any power on earth except themselves. "We are actually in a situation of revolution and discord, when it becomes the duty of every individual to protect himself." Unless the Texans did something, he continued, the mandates of every officer in the republic and state would be trampled underfoot. He concluded by placing the responsibility for calling the convention squarely on Smith's shoulders: "You, as the highest legal and constitutional officer in the State and the only one in existence that we ought to obey, have it in your power to do everything for Texas, by taking the lead in our public affairs."[3]

On October 20, Smith acted on Travis' advice by publishing an address to the *ayuntamientos* and to the populace. He called for elections in the various districts to select delegates to a constitutional assembly. He left the site of the meeting up to the Central Committee, but he obviously assumed that it would be at San Felipe. He also urged that the Anglo-Texans move in concert with Mexican states' rightists as their greatest hope of success. And many of the Mexicans in Texas did seem ready to move in the same direction. In October the leading Mexican citizens at Bexar sent an invitation to the political chiefs of all departments calling for an election of delegates to meet in Bexar on November 15. Thus the Mexican and Anglo leadership, or at least some of it, seemed to be in agreement. Travis warned Smith that not everyone in San Felipe agreed with the call, but he still urged Smith to continue in step with the Mexicans as the greatest good could be accomplished by such concert, even if it was at the expense of the Central

Committee's leadership. Travis, evidencing some appreciation for the Mexican's concern for appearances, was content to let the *ayunatamiento* at Bexar have the lead if the outcome was the same—independent statehood. Meanwhile he had to turn to other matters. His term as secretary was coming to an end, and the convening of court in San Felipe demanded a portion of his time. He continued to urge Smith to come to San Felipe because he felt that Smith's presence there would keep down the opposition. But Smith did not come, and the Central Committee, meeting in San Felipe, snatched the pot from the fire before it could boil. The committee, composed of Miller, Peebles, Johnson, Martin, Pettus, Williamson, Jack and Travis, voted to publish a broadside denying the necessity for the convention which had been called for November 15. The committee did so because things were apparently going along smoothly and because they feared the convention would endanger Austin, who was still in Mexico.

Travis had grossly miscalculated public opinion, for he obviously anticipated that the Anglo citizens of Texas were ready to complete what they had begun in 1833 and what they had sent Austin to Mexico to obtain. Now that Austin had passed immediate danger, and Smith had gone so far as to call the Anglos to a convention at the same time the Mexican element at Bexar was ready to move, Travis must have been sorely disappointed at the committee's action. Travis was not always in step with his fellow Anglos, however. Often in the pressing for statehood and independence in front of them, he sometimes would render himself unpopular with the more cautious. Now he had need to explain himself to Smith, whom he had helped draw into an exposed position. In a letter to Henry Smith on November 4, he begged forgiveness for his delay in communicating an explanation of San Felipe's denial of the Political Chief's call, blaming the tardiness on the press of court business. This was probably accurate but it was also a convenient excuse for the delay of an unpleasant task.

He assured Smith that he had circulated his proclamation but that public opinion there ran against the election of delegates and the convention. The majority of the committee were against the move, said Travis, and it seemed useless to oppose them. "Indeed, unless the people were more favorable to the plan than they are here, I should say let us remain quiet," and further on, "It is not a faction that are opposed to organizing. In this jurisdiction it is the people, and that almost unanimously." He concluded, "I am sorry that public opinion is so much against my own, but when I know and feel that it is, I can but submit."[4]

Disregarding Travis' new advice about the feeling of the Brazos Department and the farmers generally, Smith decided to push ahead. He wrote to Juan Seguin at San Antonio asking him to delay the convention until elections could be held, then he urged the Brazos district to select its delegates. But as Travis had warned him, disappointment was the only result of his efforts. Few ballots were actually cast, and the majority of those were against sending delegates at that time. Smith was upset by the outcome of the election; he published a broadside attacking the Central Committee for their lack of cooperation and dispatched an angry letter to Travis blaming him and the committee for perpetrating a state of anarchy and contributing to military misrule.[5] Travis, usually quick to anger, took Smith's letter in stride. He acknowledged that the committee had blocked the statehood convention, but, he claimed, "it could not be helped. My voice in the committee was only one against six." Recognizing the inevitable, he had acquiesed. "I found myself alone. All my friends were opposed to my views. I could do nothing buy yield to the voice of the majority, no matter what my individual opinion was, and that opinion you have long since had, for I have never had but one on the subject of a State . . . ."[6]

Some of the fault may have lain with the personality of Smith. Not a member of the committee and not associated with the San Felipe leadership, he had been appointed to a political position over them despite their recommendation of others. Perhaps if he had heeded Travis' advice and spent more time in San Felipe he would have understood the situation there or have been in a better position to change it. For the time being, the statehood idea had to be set aside, and with it the leadership of Smith, and because of his support of Smith, the influence of Travis as well. His term as secretary of the San Felipe *ayuntamiento* expired with the end of 1834, and on January 17, 1835, he began a partnership with T. Willis Nibbs to practice in San Felipe and Columbia.[7] The partnership, like other arrangements in Travis' life in Texas, was brief, but Nibbs remained his close associate throughout the stormy events of the summer of 1835. Travis was involved in a number of legal and business ventures in the spring of that year, including a scheme with Robert Harris to bring a coastal and river boat service to Texas. This venture ran counter to the current desires of the Mexican government, and this is a partial explanation for Travis' involvement in the second Anahuac disturbance.

The roots of this flare-up in late June of 1835 go at least as far back as the encounter with Bradburn in 1832. Travis had been the cause of that incident because he was a resident of the community and was directly involved in the protest against the actions of Bradburn. In this case his involvement, while no less personal, is far more political because of his move to San Felipe and his affiliation with the activists of that place. In this incident he is the interferer, the one who comes to deliver the sufferers at the hands of Mexican abuses, and his motives are far more complex.

The renewal of the trouble may be attributed to the increasing shift in Mexico to the centralists as Santa Anna consolidated his authority. Some states, including Zacatecas and Coahuila, continued to hold out against his grab for complete power. Most Texans would have been content to remain aloof from the struggle because Austin, although released from close confinement, was still a prisoner in Mexico. But the events of the spring pulled some of them back to activism, and the group known as the war party followed the events with a suspicious eye. The struggle began with the dispute over the site of Coahuila's capital and a resultant land speculation scheme. Since the centralist-state's rights argument had become acute, it had been symbolized in the north by the struggle between Monclova and Saltillo to have the seat of state government. The Saltillians were in this instance centralists, while the Monclovans reflected more liberalism and generosity in land allocation and seemed to be the localists. Santa Anna personally crushed the liberalism of Zacatecas, but he depended on his brother-in-law, General Martin Perfecto de Cos, to handle Coahuila since it fell within his command of the Eastern Provinces. Cos soon had his opportunity when the Monclova legislature in March of 1835 sought to finance its activities through the sale of 400 leagues of land. Cos declared this void on the basis of unconstitutionality, but the real consternation came when it developed that the largest beneficiaries of the renewal of land sales had been the Texas-Anglos Samuel Williams, Frank W. Johnson, and Dr. Robert Peebles. The peace group, fearing that this would cause trouble over the issue of separate statehood for Texas—the issue that sent Austin to a Mexican jail two years earlier—angrily reacted to this disclosure. Travis' reaction, that the war party should remain quiet, gave evidence of the growing division among Texans themselves in the two-way split between centralists and states' righters, and between cooperationists and separatists.

The real impact of the arrival of Cos as a major power in the Texas area was felt when it was learned that he again intended to collect customs in Texas. Cos appointed Colonel Domingo Ugartechea to command the military district of Texas, and one of his assignments was the reestablishment of custom offices on the Texas coast. Ugartechea had been a sensible, conscientious officer in his dealings with Texans in the past, but he was also a nationalist and a soldier who obeyed orders. Accordingly, he sent Captain Antonio Tenorio to Anahuac with a company of troops to aid Jose Gonzales, who was dispatched as the actual customs officer. The customs collection had been neglected after the clash with Bradburn and Fisher, although tonnage duties were sporadically collected, without incident, in the intervening months. The payment of these duties represented the recognition of the central authority to collect them, but they were apparently paid by some with no objection, paid by others when they had no choice, and avoided by many when they had the opportunity. There is little doubt that a rich "smuggling" trade was flourishing. Naturally the beneficiaries of the "salutary neglect" period were upset by the arrival not only of a customs officer with renewed authority, but of a company of unwelcomed soldiers as well. Throughout the spring clashes of personality occurred between Tenorio and the Anahuac citizenry, especially the merchants who refused him credit for supplies because of previous unpaid debts owed by the government. The center of the difficulty was Andrew Briscoe, an Anahuac merchant and a friend and correspondent of Travis. In a letter to J. K. Allen, Briscoe complained of his relations with Tenorio:[8]

> I landed at this place near 4 weeks. Since I have had some damned rough usuage, having my goods landed against my will by military force. The people would calmly stand by and see me lose all. God damn them. I went to Miloska to get justice but failed. The roughest affair and most dangerous exertions implied. My business has been delayed. My provisions and groceries have been [confiscated] as contraband and the whole duties claimed on the balance and the goods withheld till the duties shall be paid. And all this by deputy collector and 40 soldiers!!!

Briscoe and others complained about the collection of duties, and they also resented the unevenness of enforcement at the Texas ports. At Brazoria, for instance, only tonnage duties were collected, while at Anahuac and Galveston full importation taxes were levied. It was not long before the situation produced an organized response. This began as "loyalty" meetings, but some vigilante-style groups soon progressed to more overt tactics. On the evening of May 3 a band of men burned the supply of lumber at Anahuac which had been sent to rebuild the fort, and the next day a group met at Benjamin Freeman's place to discuss the event. Numbering about twenty-five, they elected William Hardin as their leader. Briscoe was there, and he presented a series of resolutions asking the government for continued tax exemption on the ground that the settlers could not afford to pay them, and further requesting that the unequal collection practices should be eliminated before further attempts to collect taxes should be made. Although adopted, these resolutions were never presented because Hardin left for the United States and the thrust for action was temporarily lost. But the momentum was easily regained when a Mexican ship, the *Montezuma*, seized the *Martha*, a schooner belonging to the firm of Harris and Wilson, a Travis retainer, as it was trying to make port at Harrisburg with a cargo of sawmill machinery, merchandise, and some passengers. The passengers who were unable to show passports were arrested and the cargo was impounded. Despite the protests of the company, the Mexican ship sailed for Vera Cruz with its prize and prisonsers, ignoring their demands that they be released because they did not know that the passports would be required.[9] Wilson informed Travis, his attorney, of these activities, and the tone of his letter clearly suggested that some retaliatory action would be desired. But the next move came from Tenorio, who, embolded by the *Montezuma's* overt actions, continued the collection of customs at Galveston despite the absence of Gonzales, the official collector. Although his commission was to help the collector, not to do the actual collecting himself, he continued in the action until Gonzales' replacement arrived on June 11. When the new collector arrived to take up his duties, he was assigned a squad of soldiers in anticipation of the arrival of Andrew Briscoe, who was scheduled to come to Galveston to pay past duties. This

111

action precipitated an act of violence which began the second Anahuac confrontation.

The incident involved Briscoe, the most vocal and active thorn for Tenorio, and DeWitt Clinton Harris. Harris arrived in Anahuac on the 10th to purchase supplies from Briscoe, and was informed that he could not remove them from the town without going through the customs procedure. He was determined to avoid this if possible. Since his mission was known to Tenorio, guards were placed around the Briscoe establishment to see that nothing was removed until the necessary duties were paid and the papers relating to the payment were in order. During the evening a young man who was evidently unrelated to Harris' business came to the store and requested a box in which he could put some ballast for a ship. Briscoe furnished the box, some bricks were placed in it, and the box was loaded on a wheelbarrow to take it to the ship. Briscoe and Harris waited watchfully to see if the box made it to the ship, and if it did they anticipated that Harris' goods might also pass. In a few minutes the young man called for William Smith, the interpreter. Briscoe, Harris, and Smith went to the place where the wheelbarrow had been stopped by the guard, who was demanding to know the contents of the box. Smith convinced him that it contained only ballast, and this seemed to satisfy the inquirer because the box was allowed to continue to the boat to be loaded. As the Americans made their way back they were confronted by a dozen Mexican soldiers, and Smith, who was evidently behind them and still moving, was shot in the right breast. Although seriously wounded he did recover. Briscoe and Harris were then jailed. Harris was released about 11 o'clock the next morning, but Briscoe was still kept in jail.[10] Tenorio's account differs significantly as to the demeanor of Briscoe and Harris. They were removing a box from Briscoe's store illegally, he reported, and when the collector and his military escort attempted to stop them they resisted. Further, Tenorio believed that Briscoe was merely trying to make fun of the collection process because the box contained only "rubbish," which he considered a maliciously planned joke. Evidently he was well aware of the Travis harrassment of Bradburn in the "Billew" incident and did not want to be dealt with in the same fashion. Travis, who was not far away, would soon be involved in this controversy as well.

Harris immediately returned to Harrisburg to carry the word of the incident, and a report was sent on to San Felipe, which was ripe for such news. While the Anahuac storm was brewing, San Felipe had also been astir. Without knowing that the latest trouble was in the making at Anahuac, but generally aware of the tensions between the war and peace groups and the way they were affected by the centralist-states' rights struggle further south, Travis was engaged in a busy correspondence with his client, Robert Harris, and with Henry Smith. On June 9 Harris wrote to Travis to complain of Santa Anna's ill-will for Texas. On the same day, Travis wrote to Smith to bring him up to date on developments:[11] Austin was released from prison; the Congress had claimed the right to alter the constitution; and a series of decrees from the State Congress had been passed, which dealt with land title disputes, the appointment of commissioners, and the permission to publish at personal expense further decrees for the general public. Evidently Travis and Smith and perhaps others were to become involved in this and similar publication ventures, for he refers to himself as the Editor and suggests that Smith and a man named Waller get such information to him. His newspaper days, although brief, would have qualified him for such an enterprise. He also told Smith that Williams, Johnson and Peebles were being detained by Cos' order in San Antonio on the charge of promoting revolution in the recent land dispute; but he was convinced that there was little immediate danger and that all should remain quiet, at least ". . . until the time . . . when we shall be called upon to act." The time was at hand.

Santa Anna turned to Coahuila after crushing the liberals in Zacatecas. Using the capital dispute and the renewed land sales as his reasons, he had Cos bring military pressure on that area. Governor Viesca and the legislature attempted to respond by authorizing a move of the government at their discretion, and Viesca attempted to get away to San Antonio. He was arrested on June 5, but others who did escape brought the news on to San Antonio at about the time the trouble at Anahuac was occurring. With the Coahuilan trouble makers in hand, Cos then could turn his full attention to Texas. Throughout the spring he had received requests from Tenorio for more assistance to deal with the violatiors of the customs duties at Anahuac. Now in late May Cos wrote that troops were on the way, and that additional support would be requested from the interior. He advised Tenorio to operate with prudence but not to tolerate any disputation of the national authority. The courier who brought this letter also carried another with the admonition, "For God's sake be firm. . . ." The bearer of these dispatches passed through San Antonio and from that city he also took Ugartechea's assurances. "Do not fail to communicate whatever intelligence you may have . . .in a very short time the affairs of Texas will be definitely settled . . .nothing is heard but God damn Santa Anna, God damn Ugartechea. These revolutionaries will be ground down, and it appears to me that we shall very soon see each other, since the Government takes their matters in hand."[12] Unfortunately for Tenorio, his commanders' letters were intercepted at San Felipe on June 21, just three days before the news of the Anahuac incident came, and they precipitated the tension into which that intelligence fell. Now they had government dispatches confirming the stories coming privately out of Coahuila. The state government was virtually dissolved and more troops were coming north. Now the peace party's urgings that orderly conduct on the part of the Texans would insure their safety fell on deaf ears.

At first chaos prevailed. Then J. B. Miller, the Political Chief, proposed the raising of three hundred men to rescue the governor and to deal with Tenorio. Although Miller would later disclaim such strong sentiments, he was evidently in the forefront of the planning. He called on the people to turn out, and his call found a ready audience when on the following day a number of representatives from surrounding settlements showed up in response to an earlier call from the Political Chief at Brazos which had been based on the unofficial reports of the Governor's arrest. But the delegates dallied and nothing was decided on the 22nd. Travis was present for these meetings, but he took no part in the plans for rescuing the Governor. Instead he favored an expedition against Anahuac. His attention was drawn there for obvious reasons; his clients were involved, and it was the scene of his former confrontation. At a secret meeting on the evening of the 22nd, the war party discussed an overt action against Anahuac. Although fear would later confuse the memories of some of the participants, especially Miller, Travis emerged with the understanding that he had been authorized to participate in the liberation of Anahuac from Tenorio's rule. On the 23rd he left for Harrisburg. There he learned that Briscoe had been released, but at a meeting held in that community on the 24th further resolutions against Tenorio were drawn up, and it was agreed that they would elect officers and head for Anahuac on the 26th. This action was delayed until the 27th, when about two dozen men gathered, chartered the *Ohio*, a forty-five ton vessel, from David Harris, and loaded a six-pound cannon mounted on sawmill truck wheels on the deck. They sailed at four in the afternoon and proceeded to Lynch's Ferry, where Travis had gone on ahead to inform David Burnet of their activities. Travis and a few volunteers joined the party there, and he was elected captain of the expedition —he later protested that the election was "casual," a good description of the entire venture—a position he had been marked for since leaving San Felipe. They reached Anahuac in the late afternoon, and the *Ohio* fired a shot to announce their presence. The appearance of a ship in the bay caused some immediate concern, but this was eased when it was learned that it was bringing more volunteers. The men landed in small boats in plain view of the Mexican soldiers, who made no attempt to stop them, and of the citizens, who had come to learn the cause of the shooting. Their arrival alarmed some of the citizens, who felt that they would only bring more trouble to the already distressed community. Travis quickly sent a message to Tenorio: Surrender.

Since night was at hand, Travis began an immediate advance on the Mexican position which was soon vacated as the soldiers sought safety in a thicket. Other Americans showed up with a request from Tenorio that he and Travis meet alone to discuss the situation. Travis was trailed by three armed men who remained in the shadows as their leader walked brazenly in the moonlight. Tenorio did not immediately appear, however, and it was only after Travis hailed him in Spanish that he spoke from the darkness of his fear to expose himself. Travis confidently approached him. Tenorio asked for an explanation of the landing, and Travis declared that he wanted the garrison's guns for the militia to prepare for the release of the Governor. Travis was not above such bombast, even though he had not advocated the latter action at San Felipe. Tenorio requested until morning to make his decision, but Travis demanded an immediate capitulation. He did permit Tenorio to consult with his officers, however, and the actual surrender was not effected until the following morning. Tenorio surrendered his arms, ammunition, and supplies, but Travis permitted him twelve muskets to use against Indians should hostiles be encountered on their march back to Mexico, and they promised not to again take up arms against the Texans.

Travis and his raiders loaded Tenorio's entire garrison on the *Ohio* and they were taken to Harrisburg on July 4th. They arrived too late for the major part of the festivities held there that day, but the barbeque was still in progress and there was to be a ball that evening. It might be expected that the Texans would be received with jubilation and the Mexican prisoners vilified by the crowd. Curiously it was almost the other way around. The peace group was yet quite strong, and they looked with suspi-

cion and fear on any circumstances which might bring
down the wrath of Santa Anna and the central government. So while the Travis command was received with no
more than cordiality, Tenorio and his group became
honored guests; indeed, Tenorio walked about shaking
hands, waltzed with the ladies, and spoke to them in
French in a gallant way. His men enjoyed themselves
nearly as much by eating their host's barbeque, playing
cards, and watching the dancing.[13]

Travis left the following day after directing that Tenorio
should be started on his march for Mexico. He arrived in
San Felipe and was immediately made aware of a shift in
opinion there, where second thoughts about his taking
Anahuac had already occurred. The feelings aroused in
late June, caused by the news of the Governor's arrest and
the plans to send more troops, had passed. The majority
of the Texans now seemed shocked that the war group,
which was still a minority, had undertaken such a danger-
ous action. It is possible that if the Mexican government
had been conciliatory at this point that the major
hostilities, now so near, could have been postponed in-
definitely.[14] The reaction to the taking of Anahuac had
begun as soon as the news of its authorization spread.
Even as Travis was still organizing his assault force the
citizens at Columbia were adopting resolutions condemning the plan. It had begun as an attempt by the war party
to get an endorsement of the resolution of June 23rd,
which they were unable to obtain. Then on the 28th
Columbia adopted a resolution which took a pacific tone.
The Columbians did request that the Political Chief
assume civilian control during the time of the Governor's
arrest, but they also urged that he should command the
people to strictly obey the laws and constitution of Mexico; and although he should raise a militia to protect them
against Indian attacks, that he was to give the government
every assurance that they wished to remain loyal and
peaceful, and that ". . .their greatest desire [was] to remain
attached to the federal government."[15]

A committee was appointed to present their resolution to the Political Chief, and the committee glossed the resolution when they reached Miller at San Felipe by also requesting that he send dispatches to Cos and Ugartechea expressing their complete loyalty. They also added a stronger plea for the formation and provisioning of the militia. As the month wore on more communities passed resolutions similar to that of Columbia, and the Anahuac group grew uneasy. Miller issued a formal apology for his June 21 proclamation and for participating in the meeting which had authorized the Anahuac venture. His actions, he claimed, had come from the excitement of the news of the Governor's arrest and the fear of Mexican troops being sent to Texas. What he seemed to say was that he thought he was supporting the government by calling out the people to militancy. When these measures satisfied neither the outraged peace group nor the Mexicans, he resigned on July 19 and Wyly Martin assumed his position. Loyalists continued in their efforts to assure the authorities of their continued affection for the Mexican system, but they also tried to explain the Texan's fear of stationing more troops in their area. And to demonstrate their loyalty they continued in their disapproval of Miller, and especially of Travis. Travis was mentioned in many of the resolutions condemning the Anahuac invasion, and the continued presence of Tenorio in Texas kept the issue current.

Tenorio had been ordered to march to Mexico with his men when Travis left Harrisburg during the first week of July, but by the 15th he had travelled only as far as San Felipe, where he was hospitably received; indeed, he was again something of a hero. Martin invited him to a public meeting held on that day to see for himself the loyalty of the Texans. They pledged every effort to return his personal property and that of the government which had been in his charge and had been surrendered to Travis at Anahuac. The length of Tenorio's stay in San Felipe was also damaging to the war party. Owing to the illness of some of his men, he remained in town nearly seven weeks where he was a constant reminder of the attack.

Completely under a cloud, Travis made a play for time. At the urging of friends, he published a card in the *Texas Republican* requesting a suspension of negative public opinion ". . .in regard to the Capture of the Fort of Anahuac, until he can appear before the public with all facts and circumstances attending the Capture of the Fort." But the explanation never came, at least not publicly. He evidently felt that he could not apologize for leading an action which had involved so many others. He doubtless felt no remorse at all; he complained to Smith that he should have remained silent because he knew that his motives were pure. He had acted by consent and approval of the political authorities and with the approval of the people, at least at the time he left. "I was only an individual actor in the business. I joined the volunteer company which had collected for the purpose of taking Anahuac and was elected its commander without my knowledge or solicitation. I see no reason why I should be singled out as the responsible person." He expressed the fear that the pledge in the card would not be accepted, however, and he suggested that Smith consult with W. A. Wharton to decide what to do. He then suggested that Smith publish the San Felipe resolutions with a few more lines of explanation in his name. "At all events let what is published be short and not in the tone of an apology, as I feel that I have none to offer."[16] Smith evidently decided not to publish anything; if he had, the result probably would have been negative. Even Travis recognized this, for in an earlier letter to James Bowie he admitted that although the people were much divided, the peace group was the strongest and made the most noise. But only a little time passed before the political wind would change and restore Travis to public esteem. As it had in 1832, his position benefited from Mexican attempts to suppress him.

While still in San Felipe, Tenorio began to pressure Martin as the new Political Chief to suppress the agitators against Mexican control, especially Lorenzo de Zavala. Martin declined on the grounds of insufficient authority, but the suggestion seemed to the peace group to be an avenue to restoring good relations. J. H. C. Miller wrote to John W. Smith at San Antonio, evidently knowing that it would be transmitted to Ugartechea, that all was then peaceful and that the best way to continue the condition would be the arrest of the troublemakers, especially Travis. He explained that while Martin was once a "revolutionary" he was now in favor of peace and that under his direction a great deal of public tranquility had been restored. "But now they [the leaders] should be demanded,—the moment is auspicious,—the people are up...Travis is in a pack of troubles."[17]

Ugartechea responded immediately by calling on Tenorio to have the *alcalde* at San Felipe arrest Travis and several other agitators. Privately he sent word that if they were delivered he would not find it necessary to enter the province to take them, but if they were not produced then that course would prove necessary. The arrest order would have come, however, whether or not Miller had made this suggestion. On August 1 Cos wrote a letter which directed just that to Ugartechea, to the Political Chief, and to the authorities in Columbia. He began with the assurance that Mexico had always drawn a distinction between loyal citizens and troublemakers, but that this latest incident gave the appearance that most Texans approved of what the latter were doing. To purge themselves of that appearance, he suggested, they needed to identify those who were disloyal and expel them. Referring specifically to Travis, he wrote, "As it is impossible that the attack made upon the garrison of Anahuac should pass with impunity I require and stimulate the patriotism of your honor to proceed immediately and without excuse to the apprehension of the ungrateful and bad citizen, Juliano Barret Travis, who headed the revolutionary party; and to cause him to be conducted to Bexar in the safest manner, and placed at the disposal of the principal commandant of the State in order that he may be tried and punished according to Law. I am informed the above named Travis is an injury to these inhabitants of Texas, and it is a shame that the public authorities should, in cold blood, be tolerating his excuses, when he ought to have been punished long since."[18] By the time these directives could be received in Texas things had changed. But still believing that the peace movement was ascendant, Travis initiated a peace movement of his own the day before Cos penned his advice to Texas. Writing to Ugartechea on July 31, Travis suggested that they open a correspondence which would enable him to explain things to the satisfaction of the authorities. The sense of his letter was that he wanted only what was best for the whole people.

While Travis waited for Ugartechea's response, which never came, the people were deciding for themselves how to address the government on their idea of their well-being. During the last days of July, representantives from several communities met in San Felipe. They rejected the idea of another convention as being too inflammatory, but they determined to send two representatives to Cos to present their peaceful desires. D. C. Barrett and Edward Gritten accepted the mission and headed west. At Gonzales they met Ugartechea's men with orders from Cos to arrest De Zavala, Travis, and several others. Fearing that this would excite the Texans as much as had the couriers in June, Gritten tried to delay the soldiers until he could get Ugartechea to change the orders. But it was all in vain because Santa Anna himself had ordered the arrest of the troublemakers. Gritten tried to communicate with Cos further, but he was informed that until the men were arrested, Cos would speak with no one about the matter.

As in 1832, the Texans could not abide one of their own in a Mexican military jail, even if he was a thorn in their side. Now the communities which a month before had been denouncing Travis and the others convened again to protest the order for their arrest. From Columbia the word was that they would not give up any individual to the military authorities, and they appointed a committee to prepare an address to all Texans requesting their attendance at a Consultation; and from Velasco came the call on the 18th of August for a Consultation to be held at Washington-on-the-Brazos on October 15th. The call was helped along by rumors and reports from the interior of Mexico that the government was preparing a major offensive against Texas to capture the offenders and to station large numbers of troops there. At this point there seemed little reason to doubt the reports, and all but the most steady peace men began to think of resistance. The mood of June was easily recaptured.

Instead of being the goat, Travis now seemed forgiven, even if he was not quite a hero. His correspondence reeks with vindication. To Smith he wrote "I am much gratified at the result of your meeting at Columbia. I hope all Texas will follow the example,"[19] and to John W. Moore, "My friend, when I returned from your place, I found the tories and cowards, making a strong effort, and for a time they were but too successful. . . . It is different now, thank God! Principle has triumphed over prejudice, passion, cowardice, and slavery. Texas is herself again."[20] And later, "I feel the victory we have gained, and I glory in it."

In other correspondence with Andrew Briscoe it is clear that Travis was thinking ahead to an ultimate clash with Mexico. He continued to gloat over the turn in fortune for him, even as he anticipated the meeting of the Consultation. He urged Briscoe to be mindful that war is not waged without means, and suggested that he actively begin to prepare the citizens in his region for the events that were sure to come. Also he informed Briscoe that already support was arriving from New Orleans in the form of men, money, and arms, including five pieces of artillery, 100 kegs of powder, and lead and shot.

With the change in public opinion Travis could now think of telling his side of the affair in fulfillment with his earlier pledge. He wrote a letter to Henry Smith, never published, which was addressed "To the Public." He excused his two month silence, which was explained privately to Briscoe and others as embarrassment, to "Circumstances beyond my control. . . ." He claimed that he was merely doing what seemed correct at the time, and that he was only "casually" elected the leader of the movement. He concluded, "I discharged what I conceived to be my duty to my country to the best of my ability. Time alone will shew whether that step was correct or not. And time will shew that when this country is in danger that I will shew myself as patriotic and ready to serve her as those who to save themselves have disavowed the act & denounced me to the usurping military."[21] At this point it would have mattered little whether the letter and its supporting documents, such as the San Felipe Resolutions, were published or not. He was as much the beneficiary of events as he earlier had been their victim. But it is too much to accept that his leadership was "casual." Because of his previous activities at Anahuac he was the logical choice to lead in this instance, he was a believer in the action, and the likelihood is great that if things had not been working his way, he would have contrived a way to be in the forefront.

Now with the momentum going his way, Travis began to prepare for the meeting of all Texans called for the fall. Despite the recent shift in opinion not all in Texas looked forward to the meeting as happily as he did. Travis wrote to others as he had to Briscoe and Moore, urging their activism in preparing the people for the meetings. But the failure of past conventions to bring much besides trouble to Texas served as an effective damper. What really helped to excite the convention movement was the news that Austin was at last returning to Texas. His imprisonment had halted the separation talk in 1833; now his return not only would revive it but would raise it to a finer pitch. He reached Velasco on September 1 and found that the meeting fever was high. He was invited to a public dinner at Brazoria on September 8 to receive the appreciation and thanks of the people for his efforts in Mexico, unfruitful as they were, and their solicitations over the fate which had befallen him in their service. The word he gave them had the ring of resistance in it. Austin had made the Mexicanization attempt more earnestly than any Texan, but he was now thoroughly an American again. He left no doubt by the end of his remarks that only the accomplished fact of Texas organization could impress the central government and Santa Anna enough to leave Texas alone. Four days later Austin was elected chairman of a meeting in San Felipe that adopted resolutions calling for the support of the Consultation by all Texans. He was also appointed to a new Committee of Public Safety. Travis was in attendance and moved that the assemblage express their appreciation for Austin's efforts. He was also active in making sure that the right people attended the Consultation. He wrote to Henry Smith that "I am extremely anxious for you to be in that convention. I want to see that body composed of men talented, firm and uncompromising."[22] And firm men were in the majority when the news arrived that Cos was about to occupy San Antonio. Austin's statement said it all: "War is our only resource. There is no other remedy but to defend our rights, ourselves, and our country by force of arms."[23] From Mill Creek Travis wrote to Austin to take the lead in arranging the time and place of the Consultation, and in whatever consequence came from it. His letter accepted fully the leadership of Austin in what was to come. He spoke of Texas being in Austin's hands alone, and of his confidence that Austin would not only accept the responsibility but administer it well. And he pledged his support.

In the first half of 1835, Travis' personal and political life had gone through several severe trials. The separation and divorce problems with Rosanna dragged on even as his relationship with Rebeca Cummings continued to warm; his son joined him in Texas, although their time together was brief, and his role in political activism brought him glory, condemnation, and finally vindication. He was a man in a stew, a man with many loose ends, and still very ambitious. Fortune, fame, and even fun, it would seem, lay before him. As he prepared for the Consultation he must have done so with great expectations. He had crossed many rivers by now — the Alabama, the Trinity and all that they meant—and only Mill Creek had slowed him down. But even that would not stop him long, for he was more than ready to go in search of other rivers.

6

Soldier

THE AUTUMN of 1835 marked the end of colonial Texas and
the beginning of a substantial consciousness of nationality. It had really been there all along, partially camou-
flaged by the attempt of many Texans to accept the conditions under which they had been permitted to come to the
northeastern Mexican provinces to reap the reward of
large land grants and renewed opportunity. Whether or
not their effort was sincere, the Mexican fears of their continued affiliation with American contacts and their support of locally disruptive forces doomed the attempt. Still,
there were many Americans in Texas who were peace
men, citizens of the Mexican system by choice as well as
circumstance, and they clung to the hope that things
would work out happily as they had done following
earlier disturbances if nothing of a further offensive nature
occurred. But it was too late. Men like Travis had carried
the thrust of resistance too far; their latent Americanism
had been suppressed too long. Now even Stephen F. Austin, the strongest voice for cooperation in previous times,
called stridently for the organization of the means of
resistance, and support of a Consultation where the statement of resistance itself could be vocalized.

The only known drawing of Travis from life.
— Courtesy Texas State Archives

Travis was ready when the call came. Under the old excuse of Indian defense, various local governments had begun the organization of the militia as early as July, and military supplies to support their activities were imported from New Orleans. Men who fight Indians can also fight Mexicans and Cos' threats to bring more troops north hit this tinder box like a lighted match. His arrival at Copano in mid-September with several hundred soldiers precipitated the further call for American militiamen. On the same day that Cos landed, Austin sent out a call for the organization of a two pronged army, one ready to take the field on short notice, and the other to be held in reserve. The rendezvous was to be at a site on the Colorado River with an alternate designated on the Lavaca, and each man was to come armed and provisioned for extended service.[1] Travis heard of the call while he was at Mill Creek visiting Rebeca Cummings, and by September 28 he was enrolled as a lieutenant in the company of Captain Randall Jones, a component of what Austin referred to as the Federal Army of Texas.[2] It was obviously an illegal, paramilitary organization under Mexican law, or the laws of any other nation for that matter, but it claimed its legitimacy as did the American forces of 1776 in its aim to defend homes and rights against what it thought to be equally illegal governmental action.

Before learning of the military call Travis' attention focused on political matters. The uncertainty regarding the meeting place and time for the Consultation troubled him, and his place of leadership in the movement meant that many people looked to him for straight answers to their questions about the meeting. On September 22 he wrote to Austin from Mill Creek, trying to persuade him to take the lead in getting the details of the meeting decided. As long as the people did not know exactly when or where the meeting would be held they could make no definite plans to attend. San Felipe and Washington were both frequently suggested, but Travis urged Austin to have the place designated "by the most competent authority we have," meaning Austin, and suggested that this would decide the matter. He concluded the letter with another pledge to Austin: "All eyes are turned towards you; and the independent manly stand you have taken has given the Sovereigns confidence in themselves—Texas can be wielded by you & you alone . . . this is not the base flattery of a servile mind—it is the reasoning of one ardent in his county's cause."[3] Elsewhere in the letter Travis assured Austin that the spirit for a war in defense of Texas was high in the minds of the people and that little effort would be required to raise troops. He must have received notice of Austin's call for troops on the 21st within a day or two, because he was enrolled in Jones company only six days after writing to Austin.

The signal event announcing the beginning of Mexican military suppression, or of the Texan's patriotic defense of their rights, depending on the point of view, occurred soon. It was an incident at Gonzales over the demanded surrender of a cannon, and it sparked the revolution and was a great aid in recruiting in the fall of 1835. Thus far the excitement was caused by the threat posed by the arrival of Cos in Texas with several hundred soldiers, still only a potential threat. Gonzales, however, constituted an overt action, and even though it was the Texans who did the first shooting, the effect was little different than that which had occurred at Lexington in 1775. It began when Ugartechea sent a small contingent to Gonzales to secure a cannon which had been placed there for use in Indian defense. Its justification instantly changed, however, when its surrender was requested. Andrew Ponton, the *alcalde*, stalled the troops by demanding written orders until reenforcements of Texans could arrive. When several Texans accumulated, they elected John Moore as their leader, and he impatiently demanded that the Mexican soldiers, instead of gaining a surrendered cannon, should themselves surrender their mission and depart. Flying a flag emblazoned with "Come And Take It," Moore ordered a volley on the Mexican camp, and the government troops retreated to San Antonio. Travis had been prevented from going to Gonzales for two reasons. In the first place he was already enrolled in, but absent from, Randall Jones' company, which was then at Fort Settlement; but more importantly, he was ill at San Felipe with influenza. On October 3rd he wrote to Jones, giving him a complete account of the Gonzales affair, including the news that Austin approved of it. He assured Jones that he would be well enough to join him in a few days, and then concluded with what may have been the real purpose of the letter: "You may say to the people of Fort Settlement —that among others—I am a candidate for the Convention & will feel grateful for their suffrage, if they believe me qualified to serve them at this important crisis."[4]

Travis' interest in the success of the Consultation had been intense since he first learned of its possibility, and it is little wonder that he would have nurtured the desire to be involved in its deliberations. The loss of public favor in July could have but dimmed his hopes both for the meeting and for his participation, but now all seemed to be going well. Like others he would be forced to decide in November if his place were at the Consultation or in the field, but now he was anticipating the meeting itself. The results of the elections for delegates did name him as one of the seven representatives from San Felipe. He was joined by Smith, Wharton and Archer, who shared his interests, and by equally interested emissaries from other districts. But the date set for the convocation, October 16, drew only thirty of the eighty or so who had been elected. Weather, harvest, and most importantly, the military service of many of the members were reasons for the poor attendance.

More formal organization of the military forces was effected in the fortnight between the battle at Gonzales and the opening of the Consultation. The men who gathered at Gonzales were in no mood for the suggestions of compromise which then came from Ugartechea; they continued in the efforts of organization. They requested that Austin come to where they were, bringing all the supplies he could muster as well as his counsel. He reached Gonzales on October 11, four days before the Consultation was scheduled to commence, and was immediately accepted as the commander. By the 16th Austin and several other intended delegates or leaders who should have been at the Consultation were instead in the army and on the move. Recognizing that important men were needed at both places, Austin urged members of the Consultation who could to join the forces in the field, but if they did not find that practical, that they should meet daily until a quorum was achieved. He also requested that the Permanent Council, or what was passing for civilian government until the Consultation could meet and establish an alternative, send men and supplies to the camp. On October 15, the day when most delegates should have assembled for the Consultation, R. R. Royall issued a circular calling for all who could to join Austin. Travis may have been responding to this call or simply following previously determined plans of his own to join Austin because he was not among the thirty who answered the roll call in San Felipe. The exact time of Travis' arrival at Austin's camp is difficult to establish; he was not listed among those attending a council of war on the 18th, at which it was determined that they would remain in place until they were joined by the anticipated reenforcements. It is likely that he was among the large number of arrivals on the 19th, because he was listed as present at that day's council, which determined to march toward San Antonio with the four hundred and fifty men then assembled. From the 19th of October until November 26 Travis remained with Austin or on detached duty from his forces, and his movements are easier to follow.

Sometime following his recovery from influenza Travis took time for what was probably his last visit with his son. Charles Edward Travis had come to Texas as part of the agreement between his estranged parents; he was boarded at Montville, home of David Ayres, and he attended a school which was operated there. Travis, probably on his way to join Austin, stopped for a visit with his six year old son. Charles begged a coin from his father to purchase some molasses with which to make candy. It is difficult to imagine the scene, which was his one recorded attempt at fatherly endeavors prior to his letter concerning Charles Edward written to Ayres from Bexar in March, 1836. It is not really surprising that his political letters are void of family references; but it is worth noting that politics did not entirely sweep his family from his mind.[5]

With Travis among its officer corps, Austin's army moved to within five miles of San Antonio. Austin tried to open a correspondence with Cos, which was rejected, and he distributed circulars inviting the Mexican soldiers to join him in defense of the Constitution of 1824 in the hope that it would encourage defections from Cos' command. When this failed, his council determined that their insufficient numbers prevented a direct attack, so a seige was planned to reduce Cos' numbers and supplies to force him to surrender. Since no immediate attack was planned, the elected delegates to the Consultation who were in camp grew restless to be at the scene of that action. Fearing that their departure might look like desertion to the volunteer army, they suggested that the camp vote on whether they should leave for San Felipe or remain at San Antonio. Sam Houston, who was also a delegate to the Consultation, arrived in camp on the day this was decided. He urged that the most pressing need was the organization of the government, something the Consultation was charged with, should it agree, and if the time was right, they were also to do the organizing. He further suggested that the army should retire before irreversible decisions were made and await the formal organization of the government. This cut against the grain of the volunteers, and William Jack's response, doubtless reflecting the sentiments of Travis, denounced Houston's equivocation and demanded that the army remain in place until San Antonio was taken. Austin's calm appeals produced a compromise. He suggested that, except for staff officers, those members of the Consultation who were in the field be released for duty in San Felipe unless they volunteered to remain where they were. Travis volunteered to stay with the army in San Antonio and it was not long before clashes between the two military camps would keep him busy, or before his nature and personality would bring him into conflict with equally determined men.

Moving the army closer to the outlying missions, Austin became aware that reenforcements were being passed into town. To locate and harass these movements, on October 27 he ordered Travis detached from Jones' command to raise a volunteer company of cavalry of his own. It was to number between fifty and eighty men, each armed with side arms and "a doubled barrell gun or Yager." Expecting that this might rob Jones of his command, Austin decreed that no more than ten percent of his company could be mustered into the new unit without his consent.[6] Travis' first command was intended as a scouting and reconnaissance unit, but it was also prepared to fight. Deaf Smith is the best known scout of the Texas military efforts against Mexico, but in November, 1835, Travis was his equal in these labors, and ". . . one or the other was always out. No one was more efficient in this line of service than Travis."[7]

While Travis was organizing his company, on October 27 Austin directed James Bowie and James Fannin to take nearly one hundred men and secure a site nearer town for the army's encampment. Late in the afternoon they selected the Mission Concepcion as the new location, but instead of returning to the old camp as directed they remained in what became a vulnerable position, at least until the main body of troops moved up. Matters were complicated during the night by the unannounced departure of some East Texas troops who decided to return home. When he learned of this circumstance the following morning, Austin sent a patrol after these men to get them to return to San Antonio and then ordered the remainder of the camp to move to the site selected by Bowie and Fannin. Travis' scouting party lead the line of march. The scouts easily crossed the San Antonio River, but the baggage wagons encountered difficulty and Austin sent word to Travis to hold up to keep him from being separated from the main column. Before Austin's order reached him,

however, Travis learned that some of Cos' men had attacked Bowie and Fannin, who were still at Concepcion.
Travis either did not understand the order from Austin or
he ignored it, because instead of stopping as he had been
directed he pressed on in full pursuit of the Mexicans who
were being driven back by Bowie's command. Seeing the
Mexicans in flight, Austin changed his mind anyway.
When he reached Bowie and Fannin, he urged them to pursue the enemy all the way into town if necessary, hoping
that in their confusion they would be easily captured.
Some of the other officers protested that the Texans were
too separated to be able to endure a counter-attack,
should one occur. While they argued, the moment was
lost. Little remained to be done except establish camp at
Concepcion, where they remained until October 31. On
the last day of the month, Austin moved the main part of
his command to the Alamo canal, within one mile of
town, while Bowie and Fannin kept their men at Concepcion. Edward Burleson commanded two companies at an
old mill that was within five hundred yards of the main
part of the city. The Texans held these positions until the
end of November, or for the remainder of the siege.

The long days in camp were a trial for the little army.
Although theoretically under a supreme commander, it
was actually a democratic, first-among-equals kind of
organization. This was to be expected from Texas frontiersmen, among whom there existed a number of ambitious, charasmatic personalities who kept the encampment stirring with frequent proposals for action. Supplies
were short and dwindling, and the need for additional
horses for the cavalry soon became obvious. When Austin
learned that a caravan of Mexican horses belonging to the
men at Bexar had started south on October 31, he ordered
Travis to take fifty men and capture the horses. The order
was addressed to Captain Travis, indicating that his new
command had brought with it a field promotion. The
country south of town was thinly settled and those who
were there were mostly unfriendly Mexicans. Austin
evidently worried about Travis because he sent frequent

notes regarding Travis' activities to Bowie and Fannin, who were still encamped in that general direction. On November 1 it was "I have no information yet from Travis," and later, "Travis is constantly out on some extra duty—He is now out. I expect him tonight and must send him to escort the cannon—. . . ."[8] Possibly Austin kept them closely informed so they could assist Travis if he needed their help.[9] Austin learned from Travis that he would return on November 2nd. But when he arrived it was without the horses. No explanation has been learned for his failure on this mission. He never located the horses, however, or some account of the resulting action would be available. It is likely that Travis simply made an oral report to Austin, who did not record it in his own Order-book or papers. Four days after he returned to camp, Travis wrote a terse resignation of his commission to Austin: "Believing that I can not be longer useful to the army without complaints being made, I herewith tender to your Excellency my resignation as Capt. of Cavalry."[10] It is interesting to note that James Bowie also resigned his position as acting adjutant-general, a post he had accepted only two days previously.[11] It is too much to assume that Travis and Bowie had already begun the quarrel over a conflict of command so widely reported the following year at the Alamo. It is likely that Travis returned to camp angered because he had failed in his assignment to capture the Mexican horses, someone had made a comment that offended him, and he overreacted.

Austin obviously still had great confidence in him, because he was already preparing another assignment for Travis when the resignation was received at headquarters. Austin had wanted Andrew Briscoe and Travis to stop the Mexicans from making day and night excursions to the west of San Antonio to gather cattle and grass to feed the soldiers and their horses; now he just scratched through Travis' name and let Briscoe take the order alone. Austin wanted this patrol to move to the west of town, range as far away as the Medina River and as close to San Antonio as possible, obtain information regarding reenforcements, and interfere with the mails and dispatches coming to Cos, especially in the event that he should be sent money. Austin had intelligence from an unknown source that money was being sent from Matamoros to purchase supplies. He wanted the patrols to prevent any supplies from entering San Antonio from the west, especially cattle and grass for the horses, and he gave them discretionary orders to fight if necessary to accomplish their assignment.[12] Travis' grievance was evidently over soon because he left with Briscoe on the mission as a volunteer, and in all subsequent correspondence from Austin to Travis and in reports from Travis to Austin the rank of captain is used and acknowledged. For instance, on November 9 Austin directed Fannin to take at least one hundred men along the Laredo road to intercept the anticipated convict-soldier reenforcements reportedly on their way to San Antonio. He informed Fannin that Travis was expected to be at the Salinas ranch on the Atascosa, and that he should attach Travis' party to his own because the Mexican force, he had since learned, was larger than he had originally thought. Evidently he still regarded Travis as being in his army and agreeable to accepting orders.

Travis himself received two orders from Austin on November 11, both addressed to him as captain. The first informed him of the previous order to Fannin regarding the larger enemy force, and requested that he meet Fannin at the Salinas ranch to cooperate in the action against the reenforcements. The second, evidently written after the first was already sent and from the viewpoint of new information, indicated that Austin had been informed by Harvey Birch of Travis' success in taking the Mexican horses, his original mission. No mention is made of Briscoe in this letter; indeed, it is obvious that Austin regarded Travis as the commander of the mission. Actually, Briscoe was on his way back to San Antonio, while Travis continued on the assignment. Birch reported that the horses, numbering about three hundred, were exhausted; therefore Austin directed Travis to take them to the ranch of Juan Seguin where they could be rested and fed out for future service. In a postscript he requested that four of the best horses might be brought to headquarters for immediate use, and that if necessary, Travis was to employ a few of his own men in keeping the remainder of the herd at the Seguin ranch. He concluded: "I have to thank you, and express my approbation of your conduct & that of your men in this affair—It has been creditable to yourself and usefull to the service—. . . ."[13] Austin also changed Travis' order to join with Fannin; he requested instead that he return at once to headquarters because he already had some additional service in mind.

Since there was a delay in hearing from both Fannin and Travis, Austin grew anxious. He informed the Consultation by a dispatch written on the 14th of Travis' success with the horses, but as no word came from Travis himself, Austin sent a command under Edward Burleson on a combination relief and search-and-destroy mission. Burleson was to move to the Leon and Medina River area with one hundred to one hundred fifty men to intercept Ugartechea, whom Austin feared was out trying to rescue the horses that Travis had captured, and if he could not find them he might attack Fannin. Burleson was to engage him first or give such aid to Travis or Fannin as might be necessary. Fortunately, Travis made it back to camp without further encounter with the Mexicans. Austin requested that Travis file a written report of his activities, which he later referred to the Consultation. Travis wrote the report on the 16th at the camp at Mill Station, near Bexar. He stated that he had left camp on November 5 on the scouting expedition as a volunteer with Briscoe's command which was to range west of San Antonio. While they were stopped at the Laredo crossing of the Medina River on the third day out, Briscoe decided to return to camp. Travis felt that if they went further down the Laredo road they might learn more about the enemy's intentions; so he volunteered to take a detachment of twelve men and move on west. He left on the 8th with his small command and camped that night at Salinas' ranch on the Atascosa. The following day they continued down the Laredo road, and, after travelling approximately five miles, discovered the trail of the horses that had eluded Travis on his previous assignment. It is understandable that Travis would not pass up the opportunity to redeem himself; even had Austin not cared any longer, Travis would have. Thus they continued to follow the trail until they came to where the party had encamped only two days previously. As the trail became fresher they gained confidence in the likelihood of catching up with the horses; so they quickened their pace until they arrived at the Macho, about fifty miles from San Antonio, the site of the previous evening's camp for the Mexicans. Travis deployed his small band for a sudden attack and they proceeded cautiously until after dark. His scout informed him when they were within two miles of the San Miguel Creek, which was the only water available for some distance where the horses could have been held for the night. He determined to hold off the attack until morning, because the Mexicans might be superior in number and he wanted the daylight to give his marksmen a chance to cut down the odds. He was also mindful that a night attack would have a greater likelihood of stampeding the horses. They camped for the night in a cold, drizzling rain without water or shelter. On the morning of the 10th Travis' men moved rapidly to the Mexicans' camp, which was located about seventy miles from San Antonio in a grove of oak trees on the west bank of San Miguel Creek. Two Mexican riders were out rounding up the horses when Travis ordered his small band to charge into the camp at a full gallop. They took the Mexicans by surprise and captured them without a single shot being fired. The band proved to be much smaller than he anticipated. Since the two who were out of camp escaped, they took only five prisoners, along with "six muskets, two swords & 300 head of gentle Spanish horses including ten mules." Travis sent a courier to inform Austin of the successful venture—he evidently received the dispatch on the 11th—and started the slow moving caravan east. Four days later he reached the San Antonio River at a point about thirty-five miles below the

137

town, and there received Austin's order of the 14th. He then sent six men and the horses on to the Seguin ranch. "I have nothing farther [sic] to add, than that during ten days of arduous service, all my men have had to mount guard every night, & to be on fatiguing duty during the day, without any other food than meat without salt; & that most of them have conducted themselves with a heroism & firmness worthy of the great cause of liberty in which they are engaged; & the satisfaction they enjoy of having rendered some service to their country more then compensates them for the fatigues & privations they have undergone in a bleak wilderness, amidst cold & rain."[14]

It is easy to imagine that Travis enjoyed the deepest satisfaction from the mission since it enabled him to achieve what he had failed to do earlier. Austin was grateful; he did not fail to include a reference to Travis' accomplishment in several letters to other commanders in addition to forwarding the news to the Consultation; and on the 18th he sent Travis' report to the delegates. In a letter to Burleson written on the 15th, he added a postscript: "Nine Oclock, P.M. I have the satisfaction to inform you that Capt. Travis has this moment arrived without accident having secured the Cavyard by sending it beyond the Guadaloupe."[15] In the report that went to the Consultation he commended the service of Travis and the men who comprised his party. The Consultation referred the communication to a Special Committee, and on November 27 the committee's chairman, Wyatt Hanks, made a report to the full Consultation on ". . .the favorable prospect of our army before Bexar and recommend to your Consideration our fellow citizen Capt. Wm. B. Travis for his personal worth and distinguished service, and also the Brave and patriotic men under his command—. . . ."[16]

Despite these successes in the field, siege warfare was ill-suited to the militia-style army that Austin commanded nearer town. They lacked the discipline required for such a campaign, and their informal going and coming added to his troubles, which were many. Fannin, returning from his expedition without engaging the enemy, resigned. Austin himself suffered from prolonged dysentery. Apparent relief from many of these cares came on November 18 when Austin learned that the Consultation had appointed him as a commissioner to the United States and requested that he come at once to accept the mission and leave for the east. But Austin was stubborn, and he feared what might happen at San Antonio should he leave before the issue was decided. On the 21st he organized the companies into assault units for an attack on San Antonio which he scheduled for the following day. Colonel Philip Sublett then delivered the final blow to Austin. He read a letter from Sam Houston discouraging an assault on the town; his East Texas division had voted not to participate, and Sublett agreed. Austin canceled the attack, informed the Consultation that he did not know when he could come, and prepared to continue the siege. He constantly had Travis out scouting and burning grass to prevent Mexican foragers from supplying their horses. Finally, Austin determined that he belonged in the civilian job assigned to him by the Consultation and should not continue in military command. On the 24th he assembled the men and asked those who would remain under another elected commander to be about the business of nominating their man. Approximately four hundred men agreed to do so, and they selected Edward Burleson as their commander. That evening Austin departed for San Felipe.[17] Travis remained a few days after Austin left, but he too was gone by December 5 when the force before San Antonio began its final assault under the leadership of Ben Milam, with Burleson holding some men as reserves. Travis was still there as late as November 26, when he filed a morning report with Burleson. His company was considerably reduced by then; he certified as present for duty only eight men, including himself, and he mentioned several who were absent without leave.[18]

Travis was himself absent from the Consultation to which he had been elected as a representative from San Felipe. When the necessary quorum had not been established in mid-October, a Permanent Council, which lasted only two weeks, was organized to administer Texas' affairs. The Consultation was finally established on November 3 with fifty-one delegates in attendance and Branch T. Archer serving as its presiding officer. The delegates agreed to publish causes for their actions, particularly the overt military clash then taking place at San Antonio; they began the organization of a more formal army; and they established a government under the states' rights constitution of 1824. Henry Smith was selected as governor, James Robinson was named lieutenant-governor, and a council of twelve to assist and advise them was named. Archer, Austin, and William Wharton were selected as commissioners to the United States. To handle military affairs, Sam Houston was named major-general and commander.

The army Houston was to command did not yet exist. The militia in the field did loosely acknowledge the Consultation and it would not be difficult to incorporate them whenever a real and present danger appeared. For the present they remained independent. When they had completed the taking of San Antonio, they could be easily led into other, equally independent actions. In the meantime, a committee of the Consultation worked at the creation of a more traditional army. In early December they determined to establish a regular army of approximately twelve hundred men. The first plan called for its equal division between two regiments, one of infantry and the other of artillery, with a select group of rangers to serve on the frontier against Indians. The organization, discipline, and pay resembled that of the army of the United States; a significant difference was the reward of land bounties for those who served Texas. Field officers were selected on December 7. Fannin was appointed colonel of the artillery, James C. Neill and David B. McComb were to be lieutenant-colonels, and Travis was named first major. Travis was at Mill Creek and did not learn of his appointment for some time, but when he did, it did not please him. On December 17 he wrote to James Robinson that although he had not been officially informed of the appointment he had learned of it anyway and wished to thank the Consultation for the honor they intended. However, Travis continued, he believed that he could be more useful elsewhere, and ". . . I beg leave to decline the office or if I have been commissioned to resign the same." Acknowledging that it was irregular to decline an office he had not officially received, he excused his action on the grounds that Texas needed all the time she could get to prepare her defenses. He further suggested that they give consideration to filling the now vacated position with Francis W. Johnson. "He is an old settler and has many claims to the favorable consideration of the council."[19] Because of other plans regarding an expedition against Mexico which he also revealed, Travis requested that Robinson not read the letter to the council but merely convey its intention. He also offered to prepare a formal resignation when he returned to town if it were necessary. Johnson was appointed major of artillery, as Travis had recommended.

Travis' recommendations were being considered in other matters, also, and this is the reason he declined the artillery post. In late November or early December the council requested Travis to give his opinion on the creation of a volunteer corps, including cavalry, to complete the army. On December 3 he addressed a lengthy letter to "His Excellency the Governor & General Council of Texas" in which he outlined his proposals. He began modestly, claiming that he was only offering his opinions because they were requested since his experience was limited. He endorsed Fannin's recent recommendation for a larger army than the Consultation had originally created, then promised to confine his remarks to a volunteer corps. Since some time would be required to raise, equip, and train the regular army then being established, and since the likelihood was great that some kind of field army would be immediately needed should the Mexican force at San Antonio not be taken, or worse, be greatly reenforced, he urged that the executive be authorized to accept the services of a brigade of volunteers. This brigade would be composed of two

141

regiments numbering five to eight hundred men each and commanded by a brigadier-general who was subordinate to the commander of the regular army. Field officers could be appointed by the governor and council and the company officers elected. One battalion of cavalry, composed of four companies with forty rank and file and twelve officers, and commanded by a lieutenant-colonel, should be created. He expressed surprise that the convention had overlooked the establishment of a corps of cavalry, ". . . for I consider that such a Battalion as I have indicated, is indispensible to the services of Texas during the present struggle. Do you wish to get information of the movements of a distant enemy? It must be done by cavalry — Do you wish to escort expresses? Guard Baggage while on the road? Charge a defeated & retreating enemy? Cut off supplies of the enemy? Harrass an invading army by hanging upon his rear, or forming ambuscades in his front? Do you wish to carry the war into the enemie's country as has been indicated: Do you wish to take him by surprise, or perform any other movement requiring celerity & promptness? All these things must be done by cavalry — and cavalry alone."[20] Travis continued to instruct the council in military matters, despite his alleged lack of experience. He suggested, for instance, that the arms of the cavalry should be broad swords, pistols and double barrelled shot guns or yagers; the volunteer infantry should also have rifles; and all should be mustered into the service for at least twelve months unless the war should end sooner. Above all, they must be disciplined according to traditional rules of war, because ". . . a mob can do wonders in a sudden burst of patriotism or of passion, but cannot be depended on, as soldiers for a campaign—. . . ." Taking Travis' recommendation into consideration — indeed, his was the deciding impulse — the military committee took up the matter of the volunteer brigade and the cavalry on December 4, and on the 16th chairman Wyatt Hanks presented a report closely following Travis' recommendations.[21] Houston and Austin had both seconded Travis' recommendation for the creation of the cavalry; and with only a few changes, as in the prescribed arms, and with few additions, as in the prescription of a uniform, the corps was authorized. On December 21 Travis was unanimously elected lieutenant-colonel and commandant of the cavalry of the volunteer army. Three days later Governor Henry Smith issued his commission. It was a meteoric rise in rank. He had entered the service on September 28 as a lieutenant, organized a scouting company and served as its captain, turned down a major's commission in the artillery, and was now lieutenant-colonel of cavalry. Undoubtedly his reason for turning down the artillery post was that he knew the other command was going to be his. There was no hesitation now. This was the kind of service he had meant when he said he could be more useful elsewhere. Although the brief history of the cavalry would not give him the kind of immediate leadership-in-action of which he knew he was capable, it would ultimately bring him to the focal point of the Texas revolution.

For the time being Travis was occupied in recruiting. Following his departure from San Antonio, the men who had remained with Burleson stormed the Mexican stronghold, as has been noted. After bitter, house-to-house fighting, the enemy had fallen to the Texans and now several hundred unoccupied men gathered around Bexar. Houston, meanwhile, also had been active. He urged the Smith government to appoint field officers and recruiters to get the regular army ready. James C. Neill was appointed the commandant of San Antonio, and various other officers, including Travis, were given recruiting assignments. Travis was left in San Felipe for this task, and it was while on this duty that he received notice of his cavalry appointment, which was added to his duties as a recruiter. He also conducted some legal business, indicating that military affairs did not entirely consume his energies. Still, they remained his primary concern, even those which did not directly involve him; he reacted eagerly to the news of a proposed attack on Matamoros by the volunteer group at Bexar.

The Matamoros scheme was proposed by Dr. James Grant. Grant's personal interest was in using the Texans to regain control of lands confiscated by Santa Anna's national government. But it also offered advantages to the Texans, apart from Grant's promises of rich personal reward. For a while at least it would have taken the war to Mexico, and it gave a mission to a force that was dwindling from a lack of activity. Travis joined the chorus of those requesting the campaign. In his letter of December 17 declining the artillery position he had added, "I hope the council will take measures to fit out an expedition immediately to take the port and city of Matamoros — . . . I intend to join the expedition if one is gotten up, unless prohibited by superior orders. . . ."[22] On the same day Travis was writing this, Governor Smith asked Houston to prepare the campaign. Houston, who was understandably reluctant to undertake the offensive and jeopardize the only presently organized military unit in Texas, nevertheless ordered James Bowie to take command of an expedition against Matamoros if he could raise enough men for the task. Francis Johnson, now in command at San Antonio, was also in favor of the expedition; in addition to urging the adoption of such a plan, he considered himself in command, should the venture materialize, because the force to be used was already substantially with him. Further confusion was added on December 25 when the Council, already at odds with Henry Smith, gave command of the expedition to Colonel James W. Fannin, a command which was to include the regular and the volunteer troops, including Travis' cavalry. Travis was ordered to join Fannin with all the troops he could bring into the field, and they were to meet at Goliad, Copano, and San Antonio. With so many commanders, it is understandable that the expedition did not accomplish anything. Owing to the conflict of command, the Council on January 6 withdrew Travis' order to cooperate and returned him to recruiting duty; in fact, for three weeks he served as superintendent of the recruiting service with headquarters in San Felipe. When the expedition finally departed from San Antonio under the command of Johnson, who was accompanied by Grant, it took with it most of the available men and supplies and left the city substantially undefended. James Neill, who commanded at San Antonio after Johnson's departure, wrote that "We have 104 men and two distinct fortresses to garrison, and about 24 pieces of Artillery. You doubtless have learned that we have no provisions nor clothing in this garrison since Johnson and Grant left. If there has ever been a dollar here I have no Knowledge of it, the clothing sent here by the aid, and patriotic exertions of the Honorable Council, was taken from us by the arbitrary measures of Johnson and Grant, taken from men who endured all the hardships of winter, and who were not even sufficiently clad for Summer, many of them have but one blanket, and one shirt, and what was intended for them was given away. . . ."[23] This was only one of several complaints about the lack of supplies in San Antonio that flowed from his pen in the next several weeks.

Travis remained at San Felipe until mid-January, 1836. He continued as superintendent of the recruiting service and as local recruiter in his own community, and he also attended to such personal affairs as dissolving his legal partnership with T. Willis Nibbs and making another arrangement with Franklin J. Starr. But the forces that would bring him to his last river were beginning to gain momentum. Houston went to Goliad to inspect the troops gathering for the Matamoros expedition and was greatly discouraged by what he discovered. He tried to persuade both the troops and the civilian authorities of its meager chance of success and of the need for more formal and organized preparations for defense. His attention was directed to San Antonio by the constant appeals from that city by Colonel Neill, who wrote to both Houston and the government of his lack of supplies and men. Accepting

Neill's judgment that the place could not be defended adequately as matters then stood, he ordered James Bowie and a band of volunteers to go to San Antonio and destroy everything usable by Santa Anna and the Mexican army should it arrive there. There seemed little doubt that Santa Anna would come; the loss of San Antonio by Cos in December was more than a sting, it was a major blow to Mexican pride. In case Bowie could not accomplish his destruction of the fortifications before the Mexicans arrived, Houston asked Captain Philip Dimitt and William H. Patton to raise a hundred men and march to Bexar if it should be attacked. Houston explained to Smith in a letter written on January 17 that he would have gone personally to San Antonio had not the Matamoros fever raged so high where he was.[24] He also requested Smith's permission to do what he had already ordered done — the destruction of the San Antonio fortification. But before Smith received Houston's request, he had already taken steps to relieve Neill because of that commander's constant requests. On January 17 he ordered Travis to take one hundred men and go to San Antonio to aid Neill. Travis, who had no more than thirty men recruited and able to go, on that day wrote to Houston requesting five hundred troops and sufficient money for pay and supplies to sustain the enthusiasm of the volunteers.[25] How Travis expected Houston to produce such reenforcements and funds, unless he anticipated the return of the men bound for Matamoros, is unclear. At any rate it was a vain hope, and equally vain was Houston's desire to have San Antonio abandoned. By the end of the month even Houston recognized that San Antonio did have a value to the defense of Texas since at least part of the army was there. Neill's and Bowie's failure to execute Houston's orders determined this, and the arrival of Santa Anna's force at the Rio Grande within a few weeks would seal the issue and determine the first major battle ground of the revolution.

Travis began his preparations for the trip to San Antonio. Despite his earnest efforts to get ready, he was embarrassed by the small number of men he had been able to recruit, and by his lack of haste, which made him appear indecisive. On the 21st he wrote to William G. Hill about an order for uniforms and equipment for his men, and he was especially concerned about his own uniform. "I am ordered off to the defence of San Antonio, which is threatened with an attack from the enemy. I shall leave in two days. Do all you can to make recruits and get the cavalry on foot."[26] In addition to worrying about his uniform, Travis personally funded the purchase of supplies for his men, including flour, twine, leggings and spurs, bridles, blankets, rope, corn, and other items for specific individuals. Travis made his departure on the 23rd, but his progress was slow. By the 28th he was at a camp at Burnam's on the Colorado River. He assured Smith that in obedience to his orders he had done everything in his power to ready himself and his men for the march to San Antonio, but owing to the difficulty of getting horses and provisions and to the delay caused by desertions, the task had been difficult. He had finally left with thirty men, all regulars but four, and ". . . I shall . . . go on & do my duty, if I am sacrificed, unless I receive new orders to counter march." He reported that affairs were "gloomy indeed" and that "the people were cold and indifferent" because of "the exhausted state of the country — Volunteers can no longer be had or relied upon. . . ." He urged Smith to effect a speedy organization of the military based on conscription of the volunteers into a regular army; also money must be raised to equip the army, because without it the war could not be carried on. "The patriotism of a few has done much; but that is becoming worn down—. . . ." The extent of his service had been extreme, he told Smith, but there is no note of self-aggradizement here. "I have strained every nerve—I have used my personal credit & have neither slept day nor night, since I reced orders to march — and with all this exertion, I have barely been able to get horses & equipment for the few men I have. . . ."[27]

The following day he wrote again from the same camp to tell Smith that he was continuing with the troops he had raised under the command of a Captain Forsythe, but would wait at Gonzales for further orders. His concluding paragraph attempted to suggest those orders to Smith, and they reveal Travis' first real hesitancy in the revolution, evidence that he was temporarily discouraged, even depressed about the prospect of defending San Antonio. Since he had not been able to raise the one hundred men Smith had requested, ". . . I must beg that your Excellency will recall the order for me to go on to Bexar in command of so few men — I am willing, nay anxious to go to the defence of Bexar, and I have done everything in my power to equip the enlisted men & get them off — But sir, I am unwilling to risk my reputation (which is ever dear to a soldier) by going off into the enemie's country with such little means, so few men & them so badly equipped. . . ." Let the men continue to Bexar under Forsythe's command and be used as they might. He would go as a consultant or in any capacity Smith or Houston desired, but not in command of such a small group, even to the extent of being continued in the recruiting service. He suggested that he might resign if his request was not honored.[28] It would be possible to interpret extreme vanity in this request. His mood on the Colorado is one of depression regarding the chances of success at San Antonio, but it does not involve his actual presence there. Travis does not appear afraid for his personal safety; rather it is a fear of embarrassment at coming in at the head of so few men. In any case he was not relieved and he did not resign; instead he behaved like the soldier he had become and followed orders.

Travis reached the vicinity of San Antonio on February 2 but he did not go into town until the following day. He had never had much difficulty in crossing rivers, but the shallow San Antonio River did trouble him. The excitement of helping to prepare the defences of San Antonio and of the arriving Mexican army would heal his depression, but for now that narrow central Texas river looked

148

terribly wide. Behind him the mightier Alabama and Mississippi Rivers, the smaller but also significant Sabine and Trinity, even the gentler Mill Creek, creased his past and their waters marked the crescendos of his life. On the other side of this river lay he knew not what. Fear told him it was disgrace at least, as when he had led the attack on Anahuac and had to regain the esteem of his countrymen by devotion to duty and by Mexican mistakes. Only a small river, it was, without his knowing it then, the most important one he would ever cross.

Travis' Last Stand by Ruth Conerly.
—Courtesy
Daughters of
the Republic of
Texas

7

Command

THE San Antonio River did not seem formidable when
Travis worked his horse across the ford and into town on
February 3. The brightness of the new day cut away the
gloominess he had felt on the Colorado and eased the anxiety that filled the hearts of the thirty men who rode with
him. On their way to the river, they passed the old
buildings of the mission San Antonio de Valero, known
for some time as the Alamo after a troup of Spanish
soldiers who used it as a barracks in the 1790s. They had
been transferred from the Pueblo de San Carlos del Alamo
de Parras, or Alamo, after the Spanish fashion and the
name passed to their new residence in Texas. It had also
served as part of General Cos' defenses in the December,
1835 siege and the subsequent assault led by Ben Milam. It
captured their attention, for every man of them knew of
those events. It was part of what called them there; now
they only looked at it, hearing and seeing through the
senses of the mind those events which had thrilled the Texans before and caused them to think little of the Mexican's
fighting abilities and much of their own. Across the river
and nearly a mile away, the town where Colonel James C.
Neill had most of his men called them on. The shallows of
the river flowed under their horses' bellies and splashed

from the thudding hooves; the water stung their skin with its coolness if it came as high as their pant legs, and without their knowing it, it claimed them for the rest of their lives. Travis was in the forefront. If he could not have a larger command, at least he would lead them in with style. The new uniform he had ordered which would have shown his rank had not arrived, and he was clad in the homemade Texas jeans which served him well on the trail.[1] His rank was evident to the perceptive eye, however, for he rode in front of them with the air of a leader. Pride had returned, and it showed. His twenty-six years left him younger in appearance than some who rode behind, but he carried a maturity and sureness of himself that transcended his years. He made straight for headquarters to report for duty with those who had resisted the temptation to go off to glory with Grant and Johnson.

Neill had been left with the command after the persuasions of Grant and Johnson had taken most of the men and supplies on their quest for Matamoros. He had been busy with the work of organizing the defense of the place as best he could with what was left. The ammunition was not adequate, but such as was available was gathered and readied. Although many of the men spent time in the town, the actual defense of the place, should it come, would be made from the Alamo mission compound, and there a lawyer turned engineer named Green Jameson supervised the preparations. The Alamo had the largest collection of artillery in the southwest, and Jameson worked the men to place the cannons along the walls in defensive positions that would command the approach to the fort. Neill had written constantly to Smith and the government men gathering at the Brazos of his need for reenforcements and supplies. So far the only manpower that had arrived had been a few men, coming in twos and threes, and the two larger groups brought in by Bowie and then Travis. Bowie's men, save for James Butler Bonham, were volunteers who followed his charasmatic leadership. Bonham, although a recent arrival from his abandoned law practice in Montgomery, Alabama, had already been

commissioned a lieutenant in the Texas army after a brief
stop in San Felipe where he helped Travis with his recruiting duties. There is a Bonham family tradition that he had
come to Texas at Travis' call, but however he came, he
would prove useful in the days ahead.[2] Bowie brought
with him the encouragement of Houston to destroy the
military installation at San Antonio, but the longer he
stayed the more he became convinced that it was a place
that needed defending. Even Neill, despite his constant
complaints of inadequate supplies, clung to the opinion
that the place could not be abandoned. Nearly all who arrived there in the next few weeks would come under the
same spell — Travis ultimately called it the "key" to Texas
and the revolution — and most who left it did so as
couriers or went seeking reenforcements. Bowie and Neill
seemed to work well together. Bowie's men followed him,
Neill's looked to their own commander, and neither questioned the other. Probably Bowie had the upper hand, but
then the whole atmosphere was that of volunteering anyway. On January 23, Neill had asked Smith for authority
to hold elections to determine officers at the Alamo, and
three days later Bonham and Bowie had taken the lead in
organizing and running a meeting of the troops to demonstrate their support of Smith. Although it is too early for a
conclusive pronouncement, this meeting may also be seen
as a statement for independence. Travis was still on his
way to San Antonio while these events were taking place,
but the sense of determination and stubbornness to hold
the place that was being established then would grip him
when he arrived.

After reporting on the third of February, Travis accepted his subordinate position quietly. No letters to
Smith were written then, and there is no evidence that he
aspired to command the fort or even that he actively advised Neill or Bowie. But he was a regular officer under
Neill's direct command, and his lieutenant-colonelcy unquestionably would have made him privy to Neill's plans.
Indeed, when Neill received word of a family illness and
made his preparations to quit the Alamo—for only twenty

days that grew into forever—it was to Travis that he turned over the command of the regular troops. These were in the minority, for most of the men still looked to Bowie for their orders. Neill intended to give the entire command to Travis, or at least that is the way Travis understood it, and probably this is the way Neill fancied his own authority. However, this quickly produced trouble, because the volunteers had no intention of following Travis, at least not yet. They asked for an election to determine who their leader was. When Travis allowed the election, they voted overwhelmingly for Bowie. Travis had little choice; the election was permitted because it would have occurred anyway. When he finally wrote to Smith to explain these affairs, he did not lose the chance to also ask for more aid. The letter went out on February 12, when the Alamo garrison mistakenly thought it still had plenty of time to entertain itself with disputed command problems.

Travis assumed that Smith was aware that the Mexican army was on its way to Texas through information supplied from James Fannin or by dispatches from Johnson or Grant. He estimated that the Mexicans had approximately four thousand men at or near the Rio Grande and that they were preparing for a war of extermination against the Americans. Since his was the post nearest to them, he assumed it would be the first attacked. "We are illy prepared for their reception, as we have not more than 150 men here and they in a very disorganized State — Yet we are determined to sustain it as long as there is a man left because we consider death preferable to disgrace, which would be the result of giving up a Post which has been so dearly won. . . ." Already the mystique of defense rather than withdrawal had gripped him. He expressed the hope that dissent had stopped within the government, so the citizenry could unite in the common cause. What a large Mexican force would mean to their lives, property, and families, he hoped, would bring them to their senses. "Money, clothing, and Provisions are greatly needed. . . . For God's sake, and the sake of our Country, send us reinforcements." He informed Smith of Neill's departure, which placed him, he said, in "an awkward" situation, and he asked for orders from Smith to clear the air.[3]

The following day Travis wrote to Smith again to explain more completely the "awkward situation" he had only mentioned the day before. Once again indicating that he was then commanding in Neill's absence, he admitted that the volunteers had not liked it and he had permitted an election to determine a commander for those men who were in the Alamo when he arrived, meaning that he had not permitted his own men to vote. The ballot had gone in favor of Bowie, he informed Smith; and, since the election, Bowie had been roaring drunk, had interfered with private property, and had released all the prisoners in San Antonio's jail. Travis priggishly claimed that only his honor had kept him there because he did not want the drunkenness of any man to become his responsibility. "I hope you will immediately order some regular troops to this place as it is more important to occupy this post than I imagined when I last saw you — It is the key to Texas from the Interior without a footing here the enemy can do nothing against us in the Colonies. . . ." The grip of the Alamo obviously tightening its hold on him still further, he went on to say that he had not solicited the command of the post; but since Neill had asked him to assume it, he would continue to do so until relieved. He concluded that he expected the enemy by mid-March.[4] Travis' version of these events was substantially upheld by J. J. Baugh in a letter to Smith written on the same day. Baugh added that Travis had refused to allow Bowie to command him, which Travis had only allowed Smith to assume, but he enclosed a copy of Bowie's order of release of the prisoners, including convicted criminals.[5]

Whatever Smith's reaction to these letters, the solution was worked out at San Antonio. Bowie's conduct, if not excused, must be seen in the light of his own life. Born in Tennessee in 1795, he had lived many places and engaged in many enterprises. Well known for his violent brawls, his name was already attached to his favorite weapon, a knife designed by his brother. Bowie lived in the cane country of Louisiana before coming to Texas, and he was active in a number of businesses, including the slave trade and land speculation. In 1828 he came to Texas, accepted the official religion, and married Maria Ursula de Veramendi, the daughter of Vice Governor Juan Martin Veramendi. He was soon a man of wealth, especially if his estate was measured in land. In 1833 he sent his family to a summer home in Monclova to escape a cholera epidemic and left on a business trip. While he was gone the disease struck down his wife and children. Since the loss of his family to cholera two years earlier he had been despondent and he often treated this malady with alcohol; a drinking bout may have been expected by the nature of his command to celebrate his victory; and finally, although he masked it well, he was already suffering desperately from the pulmonary illness that a few days later would confine him to bed. Tuberculosis is the best guess, although some have called it pneumonia and even typhoid fever. When he sobered, Bowie offered the gesture which made amends; he and Travis jointly wrote to Smith to inform him that they had agreed to a dual command, Bowie of the volunteers and Travis of the regulars, and that all orders and correspondence would be signed by both. They began the letter with "we" and both signed it. It was an uneasy peace that was strained with the arrival of the Mexicans and only partly changed by Bowie's taking to his bed shortly afterward.

David Crockett was there, and it might be supposed that he too would want a share of the command. But he remained in the shadows of this struggle, content to be only "a high private," the position he had announced for himself on the day of his arrival. Crockett's very presence in San Antonio was something of a riddle; but whatever the explanation, everyone was glad that he had come. Crockett was a folk hero of the Tennessee frontier. He had warred in state and national politics with that other prominent Tennessee politician, President Andrew Jackson. Crockett seemed to win for awhile as the Whigs rallied to him, but then they abruptly dumped him when Jackson's Democrats unseated him from the Congress. Crockett left Tennessee after dramatically announcing that he was headed for Texas. Rather than looking for a new home, he seemed to be escaping the scene of a defeat. He cut a triumphant path to Memphis and Little Rock, and was finally treated to a royal welcome at Nacogdoches. Then it was on to San Antonio, the scene of the action, and before long Crockett was using the same easy references to "liberty" as were the others. In the end, he would be among the leaders, high private or not. A careful reading of his statements in San Antonio, in speeches on the way there, and of his autobiography, would lead to the conclusion that Crockett expected a great deal from his Texas experience. It may have seemed a bit far fetched, but he obviously expected the Texans to prevail, and as a hero of the prevailing, he could again be established in United States politics, perhaps even become president. One of his last thoughts involved going home and taking the political battle straight to Andy Jackson himself. Another viewpoint on Crockett's purpose in Texas appears in a letter written by Crockett to his son and daughter from San Augustine, Texas on January 9, 1836. In it Crockett speaks as one who has come to stay: "I expect in all probability to settle on the Bodark or Chocktaw Bayou of Red River, that I have no doubt is the richest country in the world, good land, plenty of timber, and the best springs. . . . I have a great hope of getting the agency to settle that country and I would be glad to see every friend I have settle there. . . . I am rejoiced at my fate. I had rather be in my present situation than to be elected to a seat in Congress for life. I am in great hopes of making a fortune for myself and family bad as has been my prospects. . . ."[6]

Crockett fit well into the political and social structure of the Alamo. He and Bowie had more in common than he and Travis, and their age and reputations might also have put them into a personal sense of competition had Bowie's health been different. Now a man of fifty, Crockett was nearly twice Travis' age, enough to give him a benevolent forbearance. Besides, he seemed to like Travis. He wrote, "The gallant young Colonel Travis who commands the Texian forces in the fortress of Alamo, received me like a man; and though he can barely muster one hundred and fifty men, should Santa Anna make an attack upon us, . . . He will have snakes to eat before he gets over the wall, I tell you." Travis introduced Crockett to Bowie, and the two preened a bit, sizing each other up, and both decided that the other would do.[7] Travis offered Crockett an officer's rank, but that was not what he wanted. His presence was of great benefit to the others. His jokes and fiddle playing and deadly accuracy with Betsey, his famous rifle, contributed to their spirits and hopes for success in many different but equally valuable ways. With the command issue apparently decided, the garrison settled into a leisurely preparation for the appearance of the Mexican army, assured each other that reenforcements would come, and enjoyed the pleasures of San Antonio. The citizens of the city adjusted well to the successive changes in authority. They had gotten along with Cos as they had before with republican and even royal authorities, and they did so now with the Texans. Some were always more favorable with whoever was in power than with others, and even now some of the Mexican population were warmer to Travis as he went about the business of preparing his fort. He tried to visit with them, it could be suspected, for intelligence purposes; but some of his interaction was also genuine friendship, despite the fact that he is often reported as having been anti-Mexican. Like most Texans, he found much in the Latin culture that was attractive, and although he had not found a Mexican wife as had Bowie, he did have friends who were Mexican. He often stopped by the residence of J. M. Rodriquez as he made the daily trips from the fort to town; and, although it must be assumed that their conversations were dominated by military and political topics, Rodriquez at least did not feel like a man who was being abused.[8] By the time of the siege however, Travis' attitude toward the citizenry came to reflect their having a definite for-us or against-us position.

He did not depend solely on friendly conversations for intelligence regarding the Mexican army, and often his sources called for delicate handling. If a stranger did bring him information, it always had to be weighed for reliability, and he had to decide how much he could let the men know. If he reacted with fear to the reports of Santa Anna's strength or nearness it would be communicated to the men. So he sent out spies, as he called them in a letter to Henry Smith on February 13, some apparently travelling all the way to the Rio Grande.[9] And then there were the Mexicans who were constantly bringing in news. Some of them were the agents of allies like Juan Seguin, and some were family members coming to warn their relatives in San Antonio. One was Blaz Herrera, Seguin's cousin, who arrived on February 20 with the information that the Mexican army had crossed the Rio Grande two days before and that it was large and formidable. Seguin informed Travis, who at nine in the evening called a council of war in his room. Herrera personally reported what he had seen, but his information failed to impress his audience. Perhaps they believed that Santa Anna could not have moved as rapidly as he had, or that the defeat of Cos would have caused him to advance more cautiously, even if he had had greater potential for speed; perhaps they were just short on credibility for Herrera. It made little difference. Some of them were now more willing to work with Jameson in strengthening the walls, or with the parties that searched for what little food had been overlooked by the Matamoros crew; but in the end they were all committed to waiting for Santa Anna no matter when he came. And he was hastening toward them with diligence and purpose.

The march was a vigorous one for the Mexican soldiers, all of whom suffered from too little food as did the mounts of those who had them, because the Texans had burned the grass in many places during the previous fall, and the weather was changeable from wet to cold and back again

159

in that season. Despite their brief training at the Rio Grande rest stop, one of the few allowed on the long march, and their worn clothes, they were pressed ever onward in Santa Anna's desire to get to San Antonio and surprise the Texans, to punish them for the defeat of Cos, and to use their punishment as an example for all of Mexico. This is one of the truly valid reasons for the battle. The traditional argument — that Santa Anna could not bypass the men who were there and go on to the settled areas of the state because they would have constituted an armed garrison behind him and have been too great a danger — is insufficient. It is even weaker than the tradition that the Texans knowingly went to the Alamo to make some kind of sacrifice. Obviously both sides had a greater purpose there. It seems more noble that Travis and the Texans who awaited Santa Anna at the Alamo expected to win. Surely they anticipated more help in men and supplies, but they did believe they were going to win until the siege had been underway a full ten or eleven days. What was to be won for an individual defender might differ from man to man — fortune, land, political power in the new republic, even the presidency of an older one. But the Mexican leader also had something to win. He could win back the national honor which had suffered with Cos' surrender, could win confirmation of his word that he would punish the Texans for the disgrace and for their piratical behavior, could by just winning a battle against them — despite his obvious advantages — look good at home. And although he knew through his own informants how few Texans were there, he also knew that they might be reenforced. They all came to the Alamo expecting to win, expecting glory perhaps, certainly expecting vindication, but in any case, expecting victory.

Santa Anna's advance reached the Medina River on the evening of the twenty-second of February, and only the swollen river kept him from crossing and beginning the assault in the night, such was his anxiety for action. If he had been able to do so he might have caught them unaware. Little had changed in San Antonio since the Herrera report. Many of the men continued to spend time in town, and despite the rain which kept Santa Anna away, there was even a party that night. But by the following morning the town had changed. Word came in the night that the Mexican army was close, and by dawn the townspeople were scurrying about, loading their belongings on such transportation as they could find and leaving town. Travis tried to discover what had caused the previously contented citizens to become refugees, but could learn nothing. Because of this recalcitrance, he ordered that no one be allowed to leave San Antonio. Finally, by late morning, he was informed that the enemy was only eight miles away. Travis immediately dispatched a scout to find the Mexican army, and he himself climbed to the top of the town's church, its tallest building, to determine if they were within sight. Squinting eyes saw only the landscape. He left a lookout to ring the bell should anything come into view and hurried down to oversee the withdrawal of the men to the fort. Within a matter of minutes the pealing of the bell summoned him back. This time Travis was joined by several others who crowded to the church roof to see the enemy at last. But they were disappointed. Still only the landscape was found, along with an angry sentinel who protested to the doubting men that he had in fact seen the advance guard but that they had disappeared behind ground cover. John W. Smith and Dr. John Sutherland told Travis that they would ride out and see just what was going on. He agreed, and as they left it was decided that if they returned at a full gallop that they had seen the enemy. Many eyes followed the backs of these two as they cautiously rode up a slope nearly a mile and a half west of town. Suddenly they stopped, were briefly silhouetted against the horizon, and then they abruptly jerked their mounts around and raced for the safety of the fort. The road was muddy from the previous day's rain, and Sutherland's horse slid and then fell to the ground, pinning his legs underneath. Smith went back for him and together they dashed on. Having seen the front edge of Santa Anna's line, they needed no further

161

encouragement. When they arrived, Travis already had his garrison within the walls of the fort, and Sutherland found him writing a dispatch. Seeing the two scouts return had already told Travis all he needed to know — the Mexicans were there and the reenforcements were not. Not a moment could be wasted. Sutherland offered to take the dispatch since he had been injured in the fall anyway, and that would leave an able-bodied man to fight.

Travis agreed; he also ordered Smith to ride for all he was worth with Sutherland on the same mission to Gonzales. His letter was for the *alcalde*, Andrew Ponton, and it was short: "The enemy in large force is in sight — We want men & provisions — Send them to us — We have 150 men & are determined to defend the Alamo to the last." Bowie was not asked to cosign the letter. Sutherland pocketed it, and, joining Smith, rode east just in time to escape the Mexicans who were then drawing up into the main plaza of the town. Soon another rider was on his way with a similar message for Fannin at Goliad. Within the walls all hands turned to the engineering work of getting ready for the assault they knew would come. What they could not know was how long it would take.

Despite the wasted hours and even days of the past two months, the Alamo was about as ready as the men could make it, even if Travis and Green Jameson were not satisfied. The irregularly shaped compound utilized barracks, outbuildings, and the Alamo chapel; and where there were no buildings to use a palisade had been erected. Earthen platforms supported the artillery — some fourteen pieces — which outgunned Santa Anna's army's. Other than their defensive position this should have been the Texans' principal advantage. However, the guns could not be directed well from these placements, and when the assault came their usefulness was brief. The beeves were in, the corn was stored, everything else had to be done without, and now they waited. Crockett's arena of action was the palisade, the weakest spot, where his long rifle could speak the loudest with its two hundred yard carry. In the stillness of the afternoon a man could hear his neighbor breathing, perhaps hear his own heart. Eyes squinted to get a clearer view of the Mexican army drawing into the town. Suddenly the defenders' biggest piece, an eighteen pounder, blasted a cannon ball into the plaza. It harmed no one, but it did signal the beginning of their defiance in the face of an actual enemy. Although he made no mention of this particular shot in a report written on the next day, Travis probably ordered it fired. What happened next is open to some dispute. Most versions agree that someone waved a white flag and requested a truce. Santa Anna's report claims that it was the "invaders" who made the gesture, and that he responded that only unconditional surrender without further discussion would be acceptable. Texan versions, while differing on other points, at least all agree that their flag or flags were in response to one waved from the Mexican side. What happened resulted from a breakdown in the Travis-Bowie command arrangement. Thinking that he saw a flag calling for a truce, Bowie sent Jameson to talk with the Mexicans. Santa Anna would not talk to Jameson, however, and Colonel Jose Batres informed him that the army would not treat with the foreigners; they must simply surrender to save their lives. Miffed that Bowie would do this without consulting him, Travis sent his own negotiator, Albert Martin. Martin met Colonel Juan Almonte, Santa Anna's aide, and they spoke for some time. Almonte informed Martin that officially there could be no actual negotiation, but unofficially a discretionary surrender would be their only hope. Martin carried this word to Travis, whose response was to order the eighteen pounder to speak again, followed by an exultant shout from the men.

On through the afternoon and into the evening the men were mesmerized by the Mexican activities of making camp, setting up headquarters in town, deploying the troops, and beginning their entrenchments. Hardly an eye left their busyness. The night was sleepless; the morning welcome, so they could see the Mexican camp again. That day Travis tried once more to summon help. He had a real need now, a demonstrable enemy right in front of him. It vindicated Neill's pleas as well as his own, even as it questioned his judgment for being there. Travis began it, "To the People of Texas and All Americans in the World: Fellow Citizens & Compatriots—," and he knew what he was doing by appealing to a wider audience. He had written to Goliad and San Felipe, even Gonzales which was nearer, and so far he had attracted no one. Now he called again for help, and it is with the expectancy that this time it must surely come. It is true that all the San Felipe government did was order a thousand copies printed and distributed, but the letter was read in New Orleans and it helped the recruiters organize a few more troops; it travelled on and was printed in newspapers as far away as New York, Philadelphia and Boston in a matter of weeks, and it brought enough help to have more than made the difference — if they had arrived there in time. It is a letter of definace, a letter of enduring fineness that made Travis more than an obscure garrison commander in a remote and hopeless outpost in a forgotten war. It made William Barret Travis a genuine personality of the American frontier, helped bring thousands of people to Texas, helped turn a war around that a decade later led into another conflict that added one quarter of the present territory of the United States. It helped; it did not do it all, but it helped, and the battle's outcome gave it permanence. Few battles have earned so much enduring fame for the defeated. The letter spoke to the American character, a chauvinistic character, a pitying character, a fighting character. And then, as now, the inspiring appeal which follows in its entirety needs no commentary or further embellishment:

Commandancy of the Alamo-
Bejar, Feby. 24th, 1836

To the people of Texas & all Americans in
the world—

Fellow citizens & compatriots—

I am beseiged, by a thousand or more of the Mexicans under Santa Anna — I have sustained a continual Bombardment & cannonade for 24 hours & have not lost a man — The enemy has demanded a surrender at discretion, otherwise, the garrison are to be put to the sword, if the fort is taken — I have answered the demand with a cannon shot, & our flag still waves proudly from the walls — *I shall never surrender or retreat.* Then, I call on you in the name of Liberty, of patriotism & everything dear to the American character, to come to our aid, with all dispatch — The enemy is receiving reinforcements daily & will no doubt increase to three or four thousand in four or five days. If this call is neglected, I am determined to sustain myself as long as possible & die like a soldier who never forgets what is due to his own honor & that of his country — VICTORY OR DEATH.

William Barret Travis,
Lt. Col. comdt.

P.S. The Lord is on our side — When the enemy appeared in sight we had not three bushels of corn — We have since found in deserted houses 80 or 90 bushels and got into the walls 20 or 30 head of Beeves.

Travis

Albert Martin took the letter as far as Gonzales, and Launcelot Smithers carried it on to San Felipe, from whence other men and other media carried it to an America anxious for Texas news. Wherever men read it or heard about it, some of them began to get ready to answer the call.[10]

In the Alamo there was more waiting. On the day Travis wrote the letter, the full command finally came to him as Bowie took to his bed with the aggravation of his illness. The next day the Mexicans, waiting for more and

Commandancy of the Alamo —
Bexar, Feby. 24th 1836 —

To the People of Texas &
all Americans in the world —

Fellow citizens & compatriots —

I am besieged, by a thousand
or more of the Mexicans under
Santa Anna — I have sustained
a continual Bombardment &
cannonade for 24 hours & have
not lost a man — The enemy
has demanded a surrender at
discretion otherwise the garrison
are to be put to the sword, if
the fort is taken — I have answered
the demand with a cannon
Shot, & our flag still waves
proudly from the walls — I
shall never surrender or retreat.
Then, I call on you in the
name of Liberty, of patriotism &
& everything dear to the American
character, to come to our
aid,

with all dispatch — The enemy is
receiving reinforcements daily &
will no doubt increase to three or
four thousand in four or five days.
If this call is neglected, I am deter
mined to sustain myself as long as
possible & die like a soldier
who never forgets what is due to
his own honor & that of his
country —   Victory or Death.

William Barret Travis
Lt. Col. comdt.

P.S. The Lord is on our side —
when the enemy appeared in sight
we had not three bushels of corn —
we have since found in deserted
houses 80 or 90 bushels & got into
the walls 20 or 30 head of Beeves —
                              Travis

*Travis' letter of February 24, 1836, from the besieged Alamo which he
addressed "To the people of Texas and all Americans in the world."
Many writers have considered this one of the most dramatic letters written in American history. The original is housed at the Texas State
Library and Archives in Austin.*

still more reenforcements before beginning an assault, began a cannonade. About ten o'clock in the morning several hundred men advanced to a line of houses near the walls until the furious fire from the Texans' small arms and artillery forced them to seek cover. Despite the continuous firing of the Mexican cannons, no one within the walls was injured; and finally the Mexicans were forced to withdraw from the houses. In a report to Houston on the day's activities, Travis was particularly complimentary to Crockett, whom he said was "seen at all points, animating the men to do their duty." He reaffirmed his intention to hold out until the last, despite the conviction that an attack from the entire force was imminent.[11] Travis knew, and Almonte later confirmed, that this had not been a full attack; it was merely an attempt to determine resistance and to establish some new fortifications. Travis was correct in his assumption that a full attack was imminent. First, however, Santa Anna wanted to harass the garrison to make the battle go a little easier when the full attack did come. During the next several days the Mexican artillery maintained a steady bombardment. At night there were serenades and intermittent cannon firing intended to keep them awake. Twice the defenders ventured outside the walls to procure firewood and to remove by the torch some houses which gave the Mexicans cover. And inside they also worked at repairing the damage done by the Mexican firing and at strengthening their position. Only occasionally did they return the fire, or use their long rifles unless someone carelessly came into range.

It is difficult to know Travis' activities for certain during this time between his letter to Houston on the twenty-fifth of February and his several letters of March 3. Undoubtedly he talked with his officers and men about their alternatives and thought about his own future. But there is no evidence in the letters which went out on the third of March that these were days of despair or depression. It is not likely that he would have revealed this to the men anyway, even if he felt it, but he probably could not have kept it out of his letters if he were really depressed. No

168

frontal assault came then, the men were still in good spirits, and his appeals were out, hopefully working. Fannin did receive his successive appeals, but he displayed a surprising indecisiveness. He had spent many hours preparing his own fort at Goliad, now named Fort Defiance, and he was reluctant to leave it. His letter to Lieutenant-Governor James Robinson, on whom his loyalty was placed in the governmental split, also reveals a lack of confidence in his ability to command. He was the only officer in the Texas military effort with professional training, but his two years at West Point seemed ineffectual now that they were being put to the test. The appeals from Travis finally moved him to leave his supposed safety on February 25. But before he was out of sight of the fort there was trouble with the wagons, the draft animals, and the commander's confidence, so he ordered a return to his own fort.

While Travis yet hoped for assistance from Fannin, he received aid from another quarter. The summons for help had quickened the men of Gonzales. They had had their own troubles not many months before over the government's demanded surrender of their cannon, and when they resisted many men came to help them hold on to it. Now it was their turn to reciprocate, and every Gonzales man, except one, whose son was permitted to replace him, rode to answer the call. It is not likely that they expected to lose any more than the original defenders had, but with a fuller knowledge of what might happen, they did make a conscious decision to take part in the fight after it had already begun. They expected others to join them, but they went in without knowing from where the additional manpower would come. They arrived on March 3, in the darkness of early morning, conducted in by John W. Smith who helped them escape a ruse by a Mexican who nearly led them into a trap on the pretense of helping them find the Alamo's gate. Once inside they raised the spirits of the men who had by now been within the walls for nearly ten days. They brought news from the outside, hope that others would follow, and, although it was not nearly enough, thirty-two extra men, raising the roster of Alamo defenders to one hundred eighty-three. It also brought Travis back to the writing table to report what had gone on and to make what would be his last appeal for reenforcements. The first letter went to the Convention which had gathered on March 1 at Washington-on-the-Brazos. Because of the confusion at the political level, he began, and because of his ignorance of Houston's whereabouts, he would report to the Convention on the affairs of the Alamo, confining himself to what had happened since his report of February 25 to Houston. Since that time, he told them, the enemy had kept up a constant bombardment while they encircled the fort with entrenchments. Now they were within four hundred yards on the west, three hundred yards on the south in the La Villeta district, eight hundred yards to the northeast, and to the north they were at the old mill, the site of Austin's headquarters in the siege of the previous fall. Despite this encirclement, the Gonzales men and James B. Bonham had all passed through the lines that day. His walls were holding, he was entrenched on the inside, and he had suffered no casualties despite the fact that over two hundred shells had fallen inside. The men's spirits were high despite the overwhelming odds, including the likelihood that Fannin would probably never arrive, although there was a rumor to the contrary. Travis reported his frequent requests for aid from Fannin, but since he was not already there he feared he could not possibly arrive in time. "I look to the colonies alone for aid: unless it arrives soon, I shall have to fight the enemy on his own terms. I will, however, do the best I can under the circumstances; and I feel confident that the determined valor, and desperate courage, heretofore evidenced by my men, will not fail them in the last struggle; and although they may be sacrificed to the vengeance of a gothic enemy, the victory will cost the enemy so dear, that it will be worse for him than a defeat." Travis reported that he had provisions for twenty days, but that he needed approximately 500 pounds of cannon powder and 200 rounds of balls plus other supplies, and he

170

prayed that they would be accompanied by additional men. If these supplies were received, he assured them, this could be the decisive battleground of the war. The power of Santa Anna could be broken there better than anywhere else. The Mexicans' blood-red flag, token of a war of vengenance, was flying and it had only served to make the men more resolute. He concluded, "God and Texas — Victory or Death!!."[12]

Travis wrote this letter in ignorance that the Convention had declared for independence the day before. They did not receive his letter until March 6. But even on March 3, he was thinking of independence, and if he did, so must have the remainder of the men. When he finished his letter to the Convention, he wrote another to a friend, reporting the same circumstances but adding, "Let the Convention go on and make a declaration of independence; and we will understand what we are fighting for. If independence is not declared, I shall lay down my arms and so will the men under my command. But under the flag of independence, we are ready to peril our lives a hundred times a day, and to dare the monster who is fighting us under a blood-red flag . . . I shall have to fight the enemy on his own terms; yet I am determined to perish in the defence of this place, and my bones shall reproach my country for her neglect. With 500 men more, I will visit vengeance on the enemies of Texas. . . ."[13] The words of loss here are drama, not despair. As late as this date, Travis still felt that victory was possible with adequate support. But he at last perceived and admitted that it was not possible without that support.

There was at least one more letter to write, one last family matter that needed attention. He also may have gotten one off to Rebeca Cummings, but this is not known. This one, however, was intended for David Ayres, and although written on a scrap of paper, it rivals his letter of February 24 in fame. "Take Care of my little boy," it began. "If the country should be saved, I may make him a splendid fortune; but if the country should be lost, and I should perish, he will have nothing but the proud recollection that he is the son of a man who died for his country." This closed his correspondence with the outside world; the last two days his pen was still and his mind was on the problem of the Alamo's defense. Even as he sat penning the last of these communications, Travis heard from his room the signaling of the arrival of the Mexican reenforcements which Santa Anna had been awaiting. According to Travis' letter to the Convention, he mistakenly assumed that the shouting marked the arrival of Santa Anna himself in the forward camp. Having just written of his determination to fight on to victory or death, the shouting told him that one or the other was near.

How Travis responded to that ominous knowledge has caused more rhetoric and printed commentary than any other aspect of his life. According to W. P. Zuber, writing first in the 1873 *Texas Almanac* and quoting Louis Rose, the Mexican cannonade stopped about two hours before sunset and their forces withdrew a considerable distance from the walls. Zuber claims that Travis took advantage of the interlude to parade the entire garrison in single file for the purpose of addressing them. At first he was overcome with emotion, but then, regaining control of himself, he made a lengthy speech in which he outlined their circumstances, admitted the probability that they would all be killed, and encouraged them to all die fighting. They cheered. Travis then drew his sword and traced a line in the dirt which extended from one end of the formation to the other, and asked all who would remain within the Alamo and die with him to cross over the line. Nearly every able-bodied man crossed instantly, and the inactives, including Jim Bowie, were carried across by their own request. One man remained behind. As all eyes looked contemptuously at him, Louis Rose sank to the ground and into momentary unconsciousness. Then he heard his friend, Bowie, urging him to cross with the rest since he had little choice anyway. When he still hesitated, Travis orderd him passed over the wall. Rose grabbed his bundle of clothes and climbed to the top of the wall, paused for a last look at the assembled men, and then

jumped to the ground in a puddle of blood. He successfully passed through the Mexican lines; but he suffered
from exposure and thorn abrasions, some of which
became infected, and days later he stumbled into the
Zuber farm. Here he was cared for until he regained his
health, and here he told the story of the indelible line.[14]
Despite the interest in the fall of the Alamo in the next
three decades, the story was not public knowledge. It is
true that Texans were occupied with consuming events
during those decades, and it is equally true that no serious,
critical study of the action was undertaken during that
time. There are many questionable aspects of the story.
For instance, why did it take so long to emerge? It might
be suggested that Rose was ashamed of his actions here,
but this does not seem likely. After all, he told the first
people he saw. But despite the suggestion of early doubters
that there was no Rose at all, only legend, there really was
a Louis Rose, sometimes known as Moses Rose, who had
come from Nacogdoches to fight in the Alamo. The
legitimacy of his existence has been substantially proven
by the county records of the Board of Land Commissioners, who relied on his testimony in a number of cases
involving land matters for Alamo defenders' survivors.[15]
Zuber later admitted embellishing the story, adding to it a
paragraph which he claimed gave it drama. This conceivably could mean that it was really Zuber and not
Travis who drew the line. But the real drama is still there;
the line not that easy to blot out. And, as the years passed,
other evidence seemed to substantiate at least portions of
Rose's story. For instance, Mrs. Susannah Dickinson, wife
of the Alamo's artillerist, Captain Almeron Dickinson,
stated in 1876 that Travis addressed the company on the
evening of March 5 and gave each man the option of
escape. According to Mrs. Dickinson, a man named Ross
decided to take advantage of the opportunity to leave.
Spelling would have meant little to her, so undoubtedly
she is referring to the same person. The difference of two
days is, however, significant. The mood of Travis' letters
on March 3 would seem to deny this kind of somberness;

but by the fifth it could have changed. No reenforcements were there, and Santa Anna's troop deployments on the fourth and fifth made it obvious that the long wait for an assault was nearly over. It is probable that he did make some kind of speech on the fifth, and whether or not he drew a line with his sword, he made the situation plain with his words. He had no need to do more. Every man there knew the situation, and they knew the consequences of their position. But the man who wrote "Victory or Death" on so many letters was a man who would have laid it bare. And he did make speeches. Isaac Milsaps, who had entered the Alamo with the Gonzales company, also wrote a letter on March 3 to "My dear dear ones" in which he paints the same hopeful scene as did Travis' own letters. Of Travis he said, "I have not seen Travis but 2 times since here he told us all this morning that Fannin was going to be here early with many men and there would be a good fight. He stays on the wall some but mostly to his room I hope help comes soon cause we cant fight them all. Some says he is going to talk some tonight & group us better for defense."[16]

If as late as March 3 Travis was still telling the men that Fannin would come, he may have only been encouraging them; but in the morning, he may himself have also believed it. The truth is impossible to know; only the mood of his letters suggests that he was still hopeful. Finally, it matters little whether or not this famous line is questionable. Certainly there was precedent for line drawing, literally and figuratively — Pizzaro drew one for his little band before leaving Panama for Peru — and the decision line was there for every man to cross whether or not it came from Travis' sword.[17]

When the last dispatch had left on March 3 Travis told the courier that he would fire the garrison's heaviest cannon daily as a signal that the Alamo still held; when it was silent the citizens of Gonzales would know that the battle was over. On the morning of March 4 the bombardment resumed, but the Texans saved their ammunition by doing little more than the signal firing and taking sure shots.

174

Following a council of his commanders on the following day, Santa Anna determined that it was time for the final assault. De la Pena claims that the defenders had by this time persuaded Travis to surrender, and that he was preparing to do so. Realizing that the Americans' surrender prior to battle would rob him of the glory of conquest and disillusion his troops, Santa Anna ordered the attack. To make the decision seem imperative, de la Pena asserted, the Mexican commander constantly spoke of Travis' courage. At two in the afternoon the attack orders for the next morning went to the various commands, and they spent the remainder of the afternoon and evening getting ready. The orders began, "The time has come to strike a decisive blow upon the enemy occupying the fortress at the Alamo." To determine the blow, Santa Anna ordered that the attack columns should be stationed at musket-shot distance from the first entrenchments, and be ready for the charge which would commence with a signal from a bugle. The first movement would be against the north battery. The first column would be commanded by Cos, the second by Colonel Don Francisco Duque, the third by Colonel Jose Maria Romero, and the fourth by Colonel Juan Morales. The first column would carry ladders, crow bars, and axes. The men were not to wear coats or blankets or anything that would impede their charge and they were instructed to wear shoes or sandals. They were to retire early for sleep, but were to be roused at midnight to provide adequate time for forming into columns.[18]

Finally, at ten o'clock, all was quiet. This is the time that Susannah Dickinson said Travis gave the men their choice. This would have been the time for it, for now all must know that the issue was soon to be decided. That night Travis visited the Dickinsons, probably because they had a child with them. When a man has children he seems to realize that the world's problems must ultimately be viewed from their needs. He had to think of his own son and daughter then. He took a black cat's eye ring from his finger, strung it on a ribbon, and placed it around the neck of little Angelina Dickinson. With a last check of the compound completed, he retired to his quarters for some rest. His servant, a black man named Joe, shared his last sleep.

The attack began on the morning of March 6 with a shout from a Mexican soldier at five o'clock. Shots soon followed from the advancing line. Armed with ladders to scale the walls, the soldiers who had waited so long on the outside sprang into action, spurred onward by the bugle that called for the full attack. Within the walls Captain John Baugh sounded the alarm. Travis, asleep in his room, became alert instantly. He jumped to his feet, grabbed his sword and a shotgun. As he started for the door, he called to Joe to follow him. Together they raced across the yard and Travis mounted the gun placement on the north wall. A quick look was enough to tell him that the situation was gravely serious. He shouted again and again "Hurrah, my boys," "Come on boys, the Mexicans are upon us, and give them hell!," and in Spanish, *"No rendirse, muchachos'."* Just as the line reached the wall he fired his shotgun into the ranks, reloaded, and fired again. Colonel Jose Enrique de la Pena said of Travis in his diary, "He would take a few steps and stop, turning his proud face toward us to discharge his shots; he fought like a true soldier. Finally he died, but he died after having traded his life very dearly. None of his men died with greater heroism, and they all died." Travis died from a single bullet in the forehead. He tumbled down the embankment and came up in a sitting position near a cannon after the bullet struck him. He was stunned, dazed, still had a wild look in his eye, and he knew that he was dying. A Mexican officer tried to bayonet him, but Travis, with a final effort, ran him through with a sword. Joe, who reported Travis' last minutes, then fled to the barracks and continued to fire at the Mexicans. Because Travis' body was found with only one shot to the head, a story soon emerged that he had committed suicide to prevent his being captured. Anselmo Borgarra, a messenger from the Mexicans of San Antonio to Juan Seguin, and Antonio Perez, their messenger to Navarro, reported that Travis shot himself when he saw the Mexicans pouring over the wall and realized that all

176

hope of saving his men was gone. Andrew Briscoe, in an account of the Alamo which was published in the *New Orleans Post and Union* on March 28, 1836, repeated the story. None of these men were present at the battle. On the other hand, Travis' servant Joe was beside him on the gun emplacement, and he stated to the Convention at Washington-on-the-Brazos that his master died fighting; de la Pena made the same claim, calling Travis' death heroic. The suicide story can be dismissed as no more than an unsubstantiated theory; the eye-witness accounts of Travis' death are plausible and are accepted as accurate.

Travis died as the third attempt by the Mexicans to get over the north wall was successful. As the enemy poured through the breech, the other defenses were abandoned; the men took refuge in the buildings, principally in the low, one-story barracks. It was then that the main struggle began. There was no communication between the men in the buildings, no unity of command: in the truest sense it was every man for himself. From doors and windows the bullets came. The gun where Travis lay was turned around and it blasted into the defenders' building, crashing through the doors and barricades. Each shot was followed by a hail of musketry and a charge, and room after room was taken; the bayonet was often used.

Bowie was found in his bed, still fighting when the enemy entered his room, and he was mutilated. One by one the defenders were overpowered. Some tried to surrender, but all were killed. The chapel was the last point taken. An officer named Evans managed to explode the magazine before it was taken; but it made little difference. According to de la Pena, seven men survived the attack and were brought to Santa Anna under the protection of General Castrillon. One of them was David Crockett. Castrillon spoke for the men, but the commander ordered them executed. The soldiers who had been in the battle were outraged at this order, but several officers near Santa Anna sprang forward with drawn sabres to execute it. Hoping to court his favor, the officers tortured the seven men before they were finally killed.

177

Mercifully, it was over soon. By half past six the firing had stopped. As the Mexican soldiers regrouped in and around the Alamo, Santa Anna came for a personal inspection. He dispatched word of the victory to the government, and his report was replete with satisfaction and vindication. He asked a black servant named Ben who was with his company to identify the bodies of Travis, Crockett and Bowie to be certain that they were dead. Later in the day Francisco Ruiz, San Antonio's *alcalde*, was told to bury the Mexican dead, confirm again the identity of the commanders, and then get wood and burn the bodies of the Americans. Mrs. Dickinson, her daughter, and Ben were summoned, told to carry the story to Gonzales and to the other Americans in Texas that the Alamo had fallen and that they would be treated the same as its defenders if they did not lay down their arms. Mrs. Dickinson saw Travis' body as she left. It was burned along with the rest. A year later when an honor party came to provide a more traditional memorial service, only ashes and debris could be found.

In the days that followed, the story of the Alamo spread eastward. It frightened and it inspired the hearers until it became the symbol of the American presence in Texas. Although a tactical defeat, it became a strategic victory — it crystalized the American concept of themselves and their title to the land, to their liberty, to their self-respect. Newspapers in the United States spoke of it, people buzzed with it on the streets, saw in it, perhaps mistakenly, perhaps not, the continuation of their own revolutionary ideals. These men were their own, and they felt the loss. The *Port Gibson Correspondent* published a letter to the editor from a friend written from Wharton's Plantation, Texas on March 31 which began with a fitting epitaph for them all: "The garrison of the Alamo of Bexar have immortalized themselves. Col. Travis, who commanded, was a man of transcendant talents."[19] Travis and the others had indeed transcended the obvious defeat. Not a forgotten *beau geste*, his and their actions at the Alamo lifted them to a long remembered place in history, and not just in Texas. All of America was gripped by the story, and many Americans came to see and possess the land they fought for. They stayed and made it a part of the United States.

It is easy to lose Travis when the story grows larger, to forget the individual in the memory of the whole body. And ironically, it is easier to remember this last part of his life and to forget its beginning, its seasoning in South Carolina, Alabama, Anahuac, and San Felipe, easy to forget the unhappiness of his life with Rosanna or the hope of his new romance. But it was all there, in him, for he was the sum of it. His life in those first years was the making of him, for he remained to the end what he had become through youth and maturity in a frontier time — an American, a man, a Travis. His ancestor Travers had crossed the English channel to gain victorious conquest, "as one chief rol'd among the rest." He had crossed many rivers himself to be a chief, a conqueror, even. The Alabama, the Mississippi, the Sabine, and finally the San Antonio, as permanent as time, rolled on. His crossings were meaningful to him, they had been the markings of his life, but they were all behind him now. If there was one more river to cross the cold morning he raced up the cannon embankment, it was wide and deep.

English actor Laurence Harvey as Travis in John Wayne's 1960 epic The Alamo, *perhaps the most famous film about Travis. Harvey portrayed Travis as a young, arrogant aristocrat who was often more at odds with his own men than Santa Anna, but he won the confidence of the garrison and gained a hero's death.*

— Courtesy Murray Wiessmann Collection

Notes

Introduction

1. De Witt Clinton Harris to Mary Jane Harris, March 28, 1826 in Looscan Collection, San Jacinto Monument.

2. Amelia Williams, "A Critical Study of The Siege of the Alamo And of the Personnel of Its Defenders," *The Southwestern Historical Quarterly*, Vols. XXXVI and XXXVII is a published version of her thesis. The sketch on Travis is in Vol. XXXVII (October 1933), 80-90.

3. *Heroes of Texas* (Texian Press: Waco, 1964), 129-141.

4. Robert E. Davis (ed.), *The Diary of William Barret Travis, August 30, 1933-June 26, 1834* (Texian Press: Waco, 1966).

Chapter 1: South Carolina

1. As with much of the Travis story, there is controversy over his ancestry. Most of the information presented here is from the work·of Major General Robert J. Travis, *The Travis (Travers) Family And Its Allies*. The book was privately printed by General Travis in 1954.

2. For a detailed case for a complimentary line, see John Bennett Boddie, *Virginia Historical Genealogies* (Pacific Coast Publishers: Redwood City, Calif., 1952), 48-64. Neither General Travis nor Boddie are completely accurate in other aspects of the Travis genealogy, so it is possible that they share some part of the truth.

3. The patent is found in Grant Book 26, p. 437, quoted in Boddie, *Virginia Historical Genealogies*, 55.

4. Information concerning Edgefield County is from John A. Chapman, *History of Edgefield County From Its Earliest Settlements to 1897* (Edbert H. Aull: Newberry, S.C., 1897; and second edition by Advertizer Press: Edgefield, 1963), esp. pages 5-10, 366-68.

5. Information on The Saluda Old Town Treaty is from *Saluda County Scene And Story* (Saluda County Tricentennial Commission: Saluda, S.C., 1970), 5-9; see also Chapman, *History of Edgefield County*, 10.

6. Edgefield County Deed Book, Vol. 14 (1797).

7. Edgefield County Deed Book, Vol. 22 (1802).

8. The letter of administration and an inventory of Barret Travis' estate are in Edgefield County Records, box 29, package 1025.

9. Chapman, *History of Edgefield County*, 74.

10. The best account of this story is in Chapman, *History of Edgefield County*, 74-75.

11. Mark A. Travis to Samuel Asbury, October 14, 1924, copy in the Looscan Collection, San Jacinto Monument.

12. Homer S. Thrall, *A Pictorial History of Texas From The Earliest Visits of European Adventures to A.D. 1879* (N. D. Thompson: St. Louis, 1879), 627.

13. DeWitt Clinton Baker, *A Texas Scrap-Book Made up of The History, Biography and Miscellany of Texas And Its People* (The Steck Company: Austin, 1935). This is a facsimilie of the original edition published in New York in 1875 by A. S. Barnes and Company.

14. Handwritten memoranda from a Travis descendant to the author.

15. The family Bible of Mark Travis became the property of James Callaway Travis, his youngest son, who would reveal its contents but rarely let it be seen. Samuel Asbury, for one, doubted its creditability. However, James' son, Mark A. Travis, did let John Bennett Boddie see the Bible. For a reference to the Bible see Boddie, *Historical Southern Families* (Pacific Coast Publishers: Redwood City, California, 1958), II, 257.

16. Merrill Bishop, "William Barret Travis," in Invitation to Fiesta, San Jacinto Association Pilgrimage to the Alamo, April 23, 1936.

17. Dick Naylor, "Concerning the Travises," unidentified newspaper clipping, dated June 23, 1907, in the Rosenburg Library, Galveston, Texas.

18. Travis, *The Travis Family and its Allies*, 33.

19. Ruby Mixon, "William Barret Travis; His Life and Letters" (Unpublished Master of Arts Thesis, University of Texas, 1930), 5.

20. Boddie, *Historical Southern Families*, II, 257. Boddie also used the same date in his *Virginia Historical Genealogies*, 62.

21. Amelia Williams, "A Critical Study of the Siege of the Alamo And of the Personnel of Its Defenders," *Southwestern Historical Quarterly*, XXXVII (October, 1933), 80.

22. Milledge L. Bonham, Jr., "James Butler Bonham: A Constant Rebel," *Southwestern Historical Quarterly*, XXXV (July, 1931), 124-136. See also Walter Lord, "Myths & Realities of the Alamo," in *The Republic of Texas* (American West Publishing Co.: Palo Alto, Calif., 1968), 18-25.

23. Minutes of Red Bank Baptist Church, Saluda, South Carolina.

Chapter 2: ALABAMA

1. Information concerning the route of the Travis family from an interview with William Letford, Archivist, Alabama State Archives, Montgomery, Alabama, on May 17, 1971.

2. Benjamin Franklin Riley, *History of Conecuh County, Alabama,* published by the author in 1881. For a discussion of the early history of the county see pages 19-30.

3. Pamphlet published by the T. R. Mill Company, in Alabama State Archives, Montgomery, Alabama.

4. Riley, *History of Conecuh County,* 26-29. The following description of the Travis' settlement in Conecuh County is partially based on this source, and also on a knowledge of the county and of the general history of the area and time.

5. Statement of James C. Travis to Samuel Asbury, August 12, 1907, Travis Collection, University of Texas.

6. For a description of Alexander Travis' home, now called Jay Villa after the nearby plantation of the Rev. Andrew Jay, see Mrs. Elizabeth D. Autry Riley, "Visitor Sees Travis Home," undated clipping from the *Evergreen,* (Ala.) *Courier,* copy in the Evergreen Public Library. For general references to Alexander Travis see B. F. Riley, *Makers and Romance of Alabama History* (n.d., n.p.), 96-99.

7. The best source on LaFayette's visit to Claiborne is in the Dellet Papers, in the possession of Mrs. W. E. Deer of Claiborne, Alabama, and "LaFayette's Visit to Claiborne," *Alabama Historical Quarterly,* 19 (Summer, 1957), 258-278.

8. For a good description of Claiborne in the 1820s, see Samuel Forwood to Editor, December 4, 1888, reprinted in *Monroe Journal,* Centennial Edition, December 12, 1966.

9. For biographical information on James Dellet, see Elizabeth Deer, "James Dellet" *Alabama Historical Quarterly,* 19 (Summer, 1957), 299, and *Biographical Directory of the American Congress* (Government Printing Office: Washington, 1961), 1073. Mrs. Deer states that Dellet was born in Philadelphia, but other sources, including the *Biographical Directory,* place his birth in Camden, New Jersey.

10. In 1835 Dellet began a much finer home which still stands, but Travis could not have visited it because he had been in Texas several years when it was built.

11. Travis Collection, University of Texas. Much of the following information regarding the Travis marriage and his professional activities was obtained from the Centennial Issue of the *Monroe Journal,* December 22, 1966, and its Supplement, April 13, 1969, and from interviews of residents of Monroeville and Claiborne, Alabama.

12. Gordon L. Evatt, Grand Secretary of the Grand Lodge of Free and Accepted Masons of Alabama to author, February 27, 1969.

13. Ruby Mixon, "William B. Travis; His Life and Letters," 9.

14. Winston Sessions, "History Is Retraced in State, County Since Early 1800 Period," *The Monroe Journal,* Centennial Edition, December 22, 1966.

15. Ruby Mixon, "William B. Travis; His Life and Letters," 10.

16. Statement of Ed Leign McMillan dated August 24, 1957, in possession of William Letford, Alabama State Archives, Montgomery, Alabama.

17. Rosanna E. Travis to James Dellet, September 6, 1834, Dellet Papers, Alabama State Archives.

Chapter 3: ANAHUAC

1. A portrait of Rosanna Cato Travis Cloud hangs in the Daughters of the Repub!:· of Texas Library, Old Land Office Building, in Austin, Texas.

2. Austin Papers, Department of Archives, University of Texas, Austin.

3. Applications for Land, Stephen F. Austin Colonies, Spanish Archives, General Land Office, Austin. For a typescript of these and other Travis documents, see also Mixon, "William Barret Travis," Part II.

4. Duncan W. Robinson, *Judge Robert McAlpin Williamson, Texas' Three-Legged Willie* (Texas State Historical Association: Austin, 1948), 16.

5. *Galveston Daily News,* August 15, 1939.

6. *A Visit to Texas: Being The Journal of a Traveller Through Those Parts Most Interesting to American Settlers* (Goodrich & Wiley: New York, 1834: Facsimile reproduction by The Steck Company, Austin, 1952), 90. For a brief sketch of Anahuac, see Walter P. Webb (ed.). *The Handbook of Texas* (2 vols.; Texas State Historical Association: Austin, 1952), I, 43.

7. *A Visit to Texas,* 91.

8. *A Visit to Texas,* 226ff., speaks of a "Judge" from Alabama who was looking for investment property. This could easily have been Travis.

9. Eugene C. Barker (ed.), *The Austin Papers,* (2 vols.; Annual Report of the American Historical Association for the Year 1922: Washington, 1928), II, 711.

10. W. B. Scates in "Early History of Anahuac," *The Texas Almanac, 1873* (reprinted by Texian Press: Waco, 1969), 681-691, claims that he arrived in Anahuac on March 2, 1831, and found Labadie, Jack and Travis already in residence. It is likely that he has misplaced the month or year, for Labadie claims to have arrived on that very day and in advance of Jack and Travis. It is likely that Scates arrived in 1832, and found them already there. The Anahuac he describes is considerably more "civilized"

than Labadie's, and some time passage is therefore indicated.

11. There are a number of good accounts of this background. For a look at some of the best, see Eugene C. Barker, *Mexico And Texas, 1821-1835* (P. L. Turner Company: Dallas, 1928); Barker, *The Life of Stephen F. Austin, Founder of Texas, 1793-1836* (Cokesbury Press: Dallas, 1926; reprinted by University of Texas Press: Austin, 1969), esp. Chapter XII, "Popular Disturbances of 1832," 322-347; Edna Rowe, "The Disturbances at Anahuac In 1832," *The Quarterly of the Texas State Historical Association,* VI (April, 1903), 265-299; and Ohland Morton, *Teran And Texas, A Chapter in Texas Mexican Relations* (Texas State Historical Association: Austin, 1948), esp. Ch. 6, "Affairs in Texas, 1831-1832," 137-156. For accounts of participants, see N. D. Labadie, "Narrative of The Anahuac, or Opening Campaign of the Texas Revolution," and Francis W. Johnson "Further Account by Col. R. W. Johnson of the First Breaking Out of Hostilities," appearing in tandem in *The Texas Almanac,* 1859, (reprinted by the Texian Press: Waco, 1969), 127-142, and W. B. Scates, "Early History of Anahuac," *The Texas Almanac, 1873,* 681-691.

12. Mixon, "William B. Travis," 15.

13. W. B. Scates, "Early History of Anahuac," 681-682; Morton, *Teran and Texas,* 141.

14. Morton, *Teran and Texas,* 142.

15. Andrew Forest Muir, "The Union Company in Anahuac," *Southwestern Historical Quarterly,* LXX (October, 1966), 256-271.

16. Morton, *Teran and Texas,* 143-145.

17. Edna Rowe, "The Disturbances at Anahuac," 270-271.

18. *The Texas Gazette,* May 22, 1830.

19. Mixon, "William Barret Travis," 28.

20. Morton, *Teran and Texas,* 151-153.

21. *A Visit to Texas,* 131-132.

22. Dean Tevis, "Fort on Trinity Bay," *Beaumont Enterprise,* January 17, 1932.

23. Carroll A. Lewis, "Fort Anahuac, Birthplace of the Texas Revolution," *Texana,* VI (Spring, 1968), 5-6.

24. Charles Adams Gulick, *et al.* (eds.), *The Papers of Mirabeau Buonoparte Lamar* (6 vols.; The Pemberton Press: Austin, 1968), III, 242-243.

25. There are a number of primary sources dealing with these events, especially in the Nacogdoches Archives. Bradburn's report, Piedras' report, and relevant correspondence between most of the important personalities involved, including Austin, Musquiz, Cortina, and others, is found here. See Nacogdoches Archives, especially volumes 62 and 63.

Chapter 4:   SAN FELIPE

1. William B. Travis' diary, in his own hand, is preserved in the University of Texas Archives. Difficult to read, cryptic, some of it in Spanish, it is nevertheless the best available window into Travis' mind. Robert E. Davis edited and published the diary in 1966. See Davis, *The Diary of William Barret Travis, August 30, 1833-June 26, 1834* (Texian Press: Waco, 1966).

2. Robinson, *Judge Robert McAlpin Williamson,* 16.

3. A copy of Travis' Last Will and Testament, in the handwriting of John Rice Jones, is in the Texas State Library, Austin.

4. For a review of Travis' reading, see Baugh, *Rendezvous At The Alamo,* 170-171.

5. Travis to the New York *Christian Advocate and Journal,* San Felipe de Austin, August 17, 1835. Widely reproduced, a copy is available in Olin Nail (ed.), *Texas Methodist Centennial Yearbook* (Elgin, Texas, 1934), 36.

6. Mixon, "William Barret Travis," 75-76.

7. Travis to O. H. Allen, July 15, 1833, in Gulick, *Papers of Mirabeau Buonaparte Lamar,* V, 52-53.

8. For an example of a will drawn by Travis, see Robert E. Davis, "Travis Draws a Will,"; in "Trans-mississippi Americana," edited by Mary M. Hirth, in *Manuscripts* (Spring, 1970), 113.

9. For a summary of the activities, see Wanda Louise Roark (Ledbetter), "Robert Wilson: Letters To His Son" (Unpublished M.A. Thesis: Stephen F. Austin University, 1966), 15ff.

10. Davis, *Diary of William Barret Travis*, 184.

11. For a discussion of this episode, see "The Reminiscences of Mrs. Dilue Harris," *The Quarterly of the Texas State Historical Association*, IV (July, 1900), 100-102.

12. Francis J. Haskins to Stephen F. Austin, August 15, 1832, in Samuel May Williams Collection, Rosenburg Library, Galveston.

13. This remarkable letter from Rosanna E. Travis to James Dellet, written from Natchez, Mississippi on September 6, 1834, is in the possession of Mrs. W. E. Deer, of Claiborne, Alabama, who lives in the Dellet house. Copies are also deposited in the Alabama State Archives, Montgomery, and the Texas State Archives, Austin.

14. Acts of The Annual Session of The General Assembly of The State of Alabama, No. 114, 112.

Chapter 5: POLITICIAN

1. Travis to Ramon Musquiz, May 13, 1834, quoted in Mixon, "William Barret Travis," 91.

2. Brown, *Life of Henry Smith*, 24-26; Mixon, "William Barret Travis," 92.

3. Travis to Henry Smith, October 11, 1834, in Brown, *Life of Henry Smith*, 27-29; Mixon, "William Barret Travis," 376-377.

4. Travis to Henry Smith, November 4, 1834, in Brown, *Life of Henry Smith,* 50-53; Mixon, "William Barret Travis," 101.

5. Mixon, "William Barret Travis," 102.

6. Travis to Henry Smith, November 13, 1834, in Brown, *Life of Henry Smith,* 56-58; Mixon, "William Barret Travis," 103.

7. *The Texas Republican,* February 14, 1835.

8. Andrew Briscoe to J. D. Allen, April 14, 1835, copy in MS collection, San Jacinto Monument.

9. Robert Wilson to Travis, May 13, 1835, Franklin Papers, University of Texas.

10. D. C. Harris to relatives in Waterloo, N.Y., August 17, 1835, in Hill Collection, Rosenburg Library, Galveston.

11. Robert Harris to Travis, June 9, 1835, Franklin Papers, University of Texas; and Travis to Henry Smith, June 9, 1835, in Gulick (ed.) *The Lamar Papers,* I, 204.

12. Printed in the *Texas Republican,* July 4, 1835.

13. "Reminiscences of Mrs. Dilue Harris," *The Quarterly of the Texas State Historical Association,* IV, 127.

14. Barker, *Life of Stephen F. Austin, 408.*

15. *The Texas Republican,* July 4, 1835.

16. Travis to Henry Smith, August 5, 1835, in Brown, *Life of Henry Smith,* 69; Mixon, "William Barret Travis," 404-405.

17. James H. C. Miller to John W. Smith, July 25, 1835, in "Domestic Correspondence," Texas State Library; Mixon, "William Barret Travis," 143, has a good account of this suggestion.

18. Quoted in Mixon, "Life of William Barret Travis," 144.

19. Travis to Henry Smith, August 24, 1835, in Brown, *Life of Henry Smith,* 72-73.

20. Travis to John W. Moore, August 31, 1835, quoted in Mixon, "William Barret Travis," 150-151, from *The Morning Star,* March 14, 1840.

21. Travis to Henry Smith, September 1, 1835, quoted in Mixon, "William Barret Travis," 413-414.

22. Travis to Henry Smith, September 18, 1835, in Brown, *Life of Henry Smith*, 74-75; Mixon, "William Barret Travis," 157-158.

23. Stephen F. Austin to the Columbia Committee, September 19, 1835, in *The Austin Papers*, III, 128-129.

Chapter 6: SOLDIER

1. Austin to the Public, September 21, 1835, in *The Austin Papers*, III, 129.

2. Comptroller's Military Service Records, No. 5926, Texas State Library.

3. Travis to Stephen F. Austin, September 22, 1835, in *The Austin Papers*, III, 133.

4. Travis to Randall Jones, October 3, 1835, in Travis Collection, University of Texas Archives; also published in the *Galveston Daily News*, July 17, 1921.

5. Mrs. A. J. Lee, "Some Recollections of Two Texas Pioneer Women," *Texas Methodist Historical Quarterly*, I (January, 1910), 209.

6. "General Austin's Order Book for the Campaign of 1835," *The Quarterly of the Texas State Historical Association*, XI (July, 1907), 31.

7. Moses Austin Bryan, "Personal Recollections of Stephen F. Austin," *The Texas Magazine*, III, 167.

8. Austin to James Bowie and James Fannin, October 31, November 1, 1835, in Army Papers, Texas State Library; also *The Austin Papers*, III, 225-226.

9. Mixon, "William Barret Travis," 177.

10. Travis to Stephen F. Austin, November 6, 1835, in *The Austin Papers*, III, 242.

11. "General Austin's Order Book For The Campaign of 1835," 34-35.

12. "General Austin's Order Book For The Campaign of 1835," 34-35.

13. Stephen F. Austin to Travis, November 11, 1835, in "General Austin's Order Book For The Campaign of 1835," 37-38.

14. Travis to Stephen F. Austin, November 16, 1835, in Army Papers, Texas State Library, and also published in William C. Binkley (ed.), *Official Correspondence of the Texan Revolution*, 1835-1836 (2 vols.; D. Appleton-Century: New York, 1936), I, 88-89.

15. Stephen F. Austin to Edward Burleson, November 15, 1835, in "General Austin's Order Book For The Campaign of 1835," 41-43.

16. "Report of Special Committee of the Council," November 27, 1835, in Binkley, *Official Correspondence of the Texan Revolution*, I, 124-125.

17. "General Austin's Order Book For The Campaign of 1835," 53.

18. Morning Report of Captain W. B. Travis, November 26, 1835, in Austin Papers, University of Texas Archives.

19. Travis to James W. Robinson, December 17, 1835, quoted in Mixon, "William Barret Travis," 430-431.

20. Travis to the Governor and General Council of Texas, December 3, 1835, Army Papers, Texas State Library, and published in Binkley, *Official Correspondence of the Texan Revolution*, I, 162-163.

21. Eugene C. Barker, "The Texas Revolutionary Army," *The Quarterly of the Texas State Historical Association*, IX (April, 1906), 234-235.

22. Travis to James W. Robinson, December 17, 1835, quoted in Mixon, "William Barret Travis," 430-431.

23. James C. Neill to Governor and Council, January 6, 1836, in Binkley, *Official Correspondence of the Texan Revolution*, I, 272-275.

24. Sam Houston to Henry Smith, January 17, 1836, quoted in Yoakum, *History of Texas*, II, 458.

25. Travis to Sam Houston, January 17, 1836, quoted in Yoakum, *History of Texas*, II, 59.

26. Travis to William G. Hill, quoted in Mixon, "William Barret Travis," 432.

27. Travis to Henry Smith, January 28, 1836, in Army Papers, Texas State Library.

28. Travis to Henry Smith, January 29, 1836, in Army Papers, Texas State Library.

Chapter 7: COMMAND

1. Walter Lord, *A Time To Stand* (Harper and Row: New York, 1961), 205.

2. Milledge L. Bonham, Jr., "James Butler Bonham: A Constant Rebel," *Southwestern Historical Quarterly*, XXXV (October, 1931), 128-129. Walter Lord questions the entire Travis-Bonham relationship, and especially this alleged correspondence, because no evidence other than Milledge Bonham's statement has been found. See Lord, "Myths & Realities of the Alamo."

3. Travis to Henry Smith, February 12, 1836, Army Papers, Texas State Library.

4. Travis to Henry Smith, February 13, 1836, Army Papers, Texas State Library.

5. J. J. Baugh to Henry Smith, February 13, 1836, Army Papers, Texas State Library.

6. For an account of David Crockett's life, see James A. Shackford, *David Crockett, The Man And The Legend* (Pemberton Press: Austin, 1968), and *Davy Crockett's Own Story As Written By Himself* (Citidel Press: New York, 1955).

7. *Crockett's Own Story*, 348-350.

8. J. M. Rodriquez, *Memoirs of Early Texas* (n.p.: San Antonio, 1913), 7, quoted in Mixon, "William Barret Travis," 234.

9. Travis to Henry Smith, February 13, 1836, Army Papers, Texas State Library.

10. The famous Travis letter of February 24, 1836 is in the Texas State Library, Austin. For a complete account of the battle of the Alamo and details not related to Travis, see Capt. R. M. Potter, "The Fall of the Alamo," *Magazine of American History*, II (January, 1878), 1-21; Lon Tinkle, *Thirteen Days To Glory* (McGraw-Hill: New York, 1958); Amelia Williams, "A Critical Study of the Siege of the Alamo And of the Personnel of Its Defenders" (Originally a thesis completed at the University of Texas in 1930 and published serially in the *Southwestern Historical Quarterly* in 1933 and 1934); and especially Walter Lord, *A Time To Stand*, cited previously.

11. Travis to Sam Houston, February 25, 1836, quoted in A. A. Parker, *Trip to the West and Texas* (Pemberton Press: Austin, 1968), 360-361.

12. Travis to the President of the Convention, March 3, 1836, published in the *Telegraph and Texas Register*, March 12, 1836.

13. Travis to a Friend, March 3, 1836, published in *Telegraph and Texas Register*, March 24, 1836, and in Yoakum, *History of Texas*, II, 79.

14. W. P. Zuber, "An Escape From The Alamo," *Texas Almanac, 1873*, and Zuber, "The Escape of Rose From The Alamo," *The Quarterly of the Texas State Historical Association* V (July, 1901), 1-11.

15. This has been well documented by R. B. Blake, a clerk in the Nacogdoches County Court House. See Blake Collection, Stephen F. Austin State University Library.

16. Issac Milsaps to Family, March 3, 1836, in William B. Bates Collection, the University of Houston.

17. For an emotional but typical Texas position on the drawing of the Alamo line, none compares to J. Frank Dobie, "The Line That Travis Drew," *Texas Folk-Lore Society Publications, XV, In The Shadow of History* (Texas Folklore Society: Hatboro, Pa. 1966), 9-16. On page 14, one paragraph states it well: "It is a line that nor all the piety nor wit or research will ever blot out. it is a Grand Canyon cut into the bedrock of human emotions and heroical impulses. It may be expurgated from his-

tories, but it can no more be expunged from popular imagination than the damned spot on Lady MacBeth's hands. Teachers of children dramatize it in school rooms; orators on holidays silver it and gild it; the tellers of historical anecdotes—and there are many of them in Texas—sitting around hotel lobbies speculate on it and say, "Well, we'll believe it whether it's true or not."

18. "General Orders of the 5th of March, 1836," quoted in *Texas Almanac, 1870.*

19. To the Editor, *Port Gibson Correspondent,* April 23, 1836, in the Department of Archives and History, Jackson, Mississippi.

Alec Baldwin as Travis in the 1987 NBC Television Network Movie,
The Alamo: Thirteen Days to Glory. *The film was based loosely on the*
book by Lon Tinkle.
— Courtesy Tony Pasqua

Bibliography

The following list of sources indicates the majority of the material consulted in the preparation of this biography. No attempt is made to rank these sources in order of usefulness or value, except in the one instance noted below, and the author's debt to these and to other sources consulted which may have been unwittingly omitted from this list is gratefully and completely acknowledged. An additional word must be said for the Ruby Mixon thesis, "William Barret Travis, His Life and Letters," completed at the University of Texas in 1930. Ms. Mixon assembled the overwhelming majority of the Travis correspondence in one useful location, and made the labor for others so much easier by doing so.

Manuscripts

Austin (Stephen F.) Papers, Texas State Library, and Department of Archives, University of Texas.

Asbury (Samuel E.) Papers, Department of Archives, University of Texas.

Bates (William B.) Collection, University of Houston.

Bexar Archives, Department of Archives, University of Texas.

Blake (R. B.) Collection, Special Collections, Stephen F. Austin State University.

Briscoe (Andrew) Papers, San Jacinto Monument.

Comptroller's Military Service Records, Texas State Library.

Crockett (George Louis) Papers, Special Collections, Stephen F. Austin State University.

Delett (James) Papers, Alabama State Archives, Montgomery, and in private possession of Mrs. W. E. Deer, Claiborne, Alabama.

Edgefield, South Carolina County Records.

Franklin (Benjamin C.) Papers, Department of Archives, University of Texas.

Hill Collection, Rosenburg Library, Galveston.

Looscan Collection, San Jacinto Monument.

McMillan Papers, Alabama State Archives, Montgomery.

Mill Company Records, Alabama State Archives, Montgomery.

Nacogdoches Archives, Special Collections, Stephen F. Austin State University Library.

Records of the Grand Lodge of Alabama, F.A.M.

Red Bank Baptist Church Records, Saluda, South Carolina.

Spanish Archives, General Land Office, Austin.

Starr (James Harper) Collection, Eugene C. Barker Texas History Center, University of Texas.

Travis (William B.) Collection, Department of Archives, University of Texas and Texas State Library.

Williams (Samuel May) Papers, Rosenburg Library, Galveston.

Theses

Mixon, Ruby. "William Barret Travis, His Life and Letters." Unpublished Master of Arts thesis at the University of Texas, 1930.

Roark, Wanda L. (Ledbetter). "Robert Wilson: Letters to His Son." Unpublished Master of Arts thesis at Stephen F. Austin State University, 1966.

Newspapers

The following newspapers were consulted directly or from quotations in other works.

Beaumont Enterprise.

Dallas Morning News.

Evergreen Alabama Courier.

Galveston Daily News.

Houston Post.

Monroe Alabama Journal.

Port Gibson Correspondent.

Saluda South Carolina Standard.

Texas Monument.

The Telegraph and Texas Register.

The Texas Gazette.

The Texas Republican.

Books

Adair, A. Garland, and M. H. Crockett, *Heroes of the Alamo.* Exposition Press: New York, 1957.

A Visit to Texas: Being the Journal of a Traveller Through Those Parts Most Interesting to American Settlers. Goodrich & Wiley: New York, 1834; facsimile reproduction by Steck Company: Austin, 1952.

Baker, De Witt Clinton. *A Texas Scrap-Book Made Up of the History, Biography and Miscellany of Texas And It's People.* The Steck Company: Austin, 1935.

Barker, Eugene C. *Mexico and Texas, 1821-1835.* P. L. Turner Company: Dallas, 1928.

_____ *Readings in Texas History.* Southwest Press: Dallas, 1929.

_____ (ed.). *The Austin Papers.* 2 vols. Annual Report of the American Historical Association for the Year 1922: Washington, 1928.

_____ *The Life of Stephen F. Austin, Founder of Texas, 1793-1836.* Cokesbury Press: Nashville, Dallas, 1926; and reprinted by University of Texas Press; Austin, 1969.

Baugh, Virgil E. *Rendezvous at the Alamo, Highlights in the Lives of Bowie, Crockett, and Travis.* Pageant Press: New York, 1960.

Binkley, William C. *Official Correspondence of the Texas Revolution, 1835-1836.* 2 vols. D. Appleton-Century: New York, 1936.

_____ *The Texas Revolution.* Louisiana State University Press: Baton Rouge, 1952.

Boddie, J. B. *Historical Southern Families.* Pacific Coast Publishers: Redwood City, Calif., 1952.

_____ *Virginia Historical Genealogies.* Pacific Coast Publishers: Redwood City, Calif., 1952.

200

Brewer, W. *Alabama, Her History, Resources, War Record and Public Men.* n.p.: Montgomery, 1862.

Brown, John Henry. *Life and Times of Henry Smith, The First American Governor of Texas.* A. D. Aldrige & Co.: Dallas, 1887.

Bryan, J. B. (ed.). *Mary Austin Holley, The Texas Diary, 1835-1838.* University of Texas Press: Austin, 1965.

Castaneda, Carlos E. The Fight for Freedom, 1810-1836, volume VI in *Our Catholic Heritage in Texas, 1519-1936.* 7 vols. Von Boeckmann-Jones Co.: Austin, 1950.

_____ *The Mexican Side of the Texas Revolution.* P. L. Turner Company: Dallas, 1928.

Chabot, Frederick C. *The Alamo, Mission, Fortress and Shrine.* Centennial Edition: San Antonio, 1936.

Chapman, John A. *History of Edgefield County From Its Earliest Settlements to 1897.* Elbert H. Aull: Newberry, S.C., 1897; second edition by Advertizer Press: Edgefield, 1963.

Cox, Mamie Wynee. *The Romantic Flags of Texas.* Banks Upshaw & Co.: Dallas, 1936.

Crockett, David. *Davy Crockett's Own Story As Written By Himself.* Citidal Press: New York, 1955.

Curtis, Albert. *Remember the Alamo.* Clegg Company: San Antonio, 1961.

Davis, Robert E. (ed.). *The Diary of William Barret Travis, August 30, 1833-June 26, 1834.* Texian Press: Waco, 1966.

Day, James M. (comp.). *The Texas Almanac, 1857-1873, A Compendium of Texas History.* Texian Press: Waco, 1967.

De Zavala, Adina. *History and Legends of the Alamo.* Privately printed by Author: San Antonio, 1917.

Dixon, Sam Houston. *Romance and Tragedy of Texas History.* Texas Historical Publishing Co.: Houston, 1924.

_____ *The Men Who Made Texas Free.* Texas Historical Publishing Co.: Houston, 1924.

Douglas, C. L. *James Bowie.* Banks Upshaw & Co.: Dallas, 1944.

Edward, David B. *The History of Texas; or The Emigrant's, Farmer's, and Politicians' Guide to the Character, Climate, Soil and Productions of That Country.* J. A. James & Co.: Cincinnati, 1836.

Fehrenback, T. R. *Lone Star, A History of Texas and the Texans.* MacMillan: New York, 1968.

Foote, Henry S. *Texas and the Texans.* Thomas, Cowperthwait & Co.: Philadelphia, 1841.

Ford, John S. *Origin and Fall of the Alamo, March 6, 1836.* Johnson Bros. Print. Co.: San Antonio, 1895.

Fulmore, Zachary R. *History and Geography of Texas, As Told in County Names.* Privately printed by Author: Austin, 1951.

Gray, William F. *From Virginia To Texas, 1835.* Gray, Dillage & Co.: Houston, 1909.

Gulick, Charles A. *et al.* (eds.). *The Papers of Mirabeau Buonaparte Lamar.* 6 vols. The Pemberton Press: Austin, 1968.

Holley, Mary Austin. *Texas.* J. Clarke & Co.: Lexington, Ky., 1836; Facsimile by the Steck Company: Austin, 1935.

Houston, Andrew J. *Texas Independence.* Anson Jones Press: Houston, 1938.

Kemp, Louis W. *The Signers of the Texas Declaration of Independence.* Anson Jones Press: Salado, Texas, 1959.

Kennedy, William. *Texas: The Rise, Progress, and Prospects of The Republic of Texas.* Molyneaux Craftsman: Fort Worth, 1925.

Le Clerc, Frederic. *Texas and Its Revolution.* Anson Jones Press: Houston, 1950.

Lord, Walter. *A Time to Stand.* Harper and Row: New York, 1961.

Lowrie, Samuel Harman. *Cultural Conflict in Texas, 1821-1835.* Columbia University Press: New York, 1932.

McCaleb, Walter F. *William Barret Travis.* Naylor: San Antonio, 1957.

Morton, Ohland. *Teran and Texas: A Chapter in Texas Mexican Relations.* Texas State Historical Association: Austin, 1948.

Muir, Andrew Forest (ed.). *Texas In 1837, An Anonymous, Contemporary Narrative.* University of Texas Press: Austin, 1958.

Nail, Olin (ed.). *Texas Methodist Centennial Yearbrook.* n.p.: Elgin, Texas, 1934.

Newell, Chester. *History of the Revolution in Texas.* The Steck Company: Austin, 1935.

Owen, Thomas M. *History of Alabama and Dictionary of Alabama Biography.* S. J. Clarke Co.: Chicago, 1921.

Parker, A. A. *Trip to the West and Texas.* The Pemberton Press: Austin, 1968.

Phelan, Macum. *A History of Early Methodism in Texas, 1817-1866.* Cokesbury Press: Nashville, 1924.

Red, William Stuart. *The Texas Colonists and Religion, 1821-1836.* E. L. Shettles: Austin, 1924.

Riley, B. F. *History of Conecuh County, Alabama.* Privately printed: Columbus, Ga., 1881.

——————— *Makers and Romance of Alabama History.* n.p.: n.p., 1915.

Robinson, Duncan W. *Judge Robert McAlpin Williamson, Texas' Three-Legged Willie.* Texas State Historical Association: Austin, 1948.

Rodreguiz, J. M. *Memoirs of Early Texas.* n.p.: San Antonio, 1913.

Saluda County in Scene and Story. Saluda County Tricentennial Commission: Columbia, S.C., 1970.

Santos, Richard G. *Santa Anna's Campaign Against Texas, 1835-1836.* Texian Press: Waco, 1968.

Shackford, James A. *David Crockett, The Man And The Legend.* The Pemberton Press: Austin, 1968.

Sutherland, John. *The Fall of the Alamo.* Naylor: San Antonio, 1936.

Thrall, Homer S. *A Pictorial History of Texas From The Earliest Visits of European Adventurers to A.D. 1879.* N. D. Thompson: St. Louis, 1879.

_____ *History of Methodism in Texas.* n.p.: Houston, 1872.

Tinkle, Lon. *Thirteen Days to Glory.* McGraw-Hill: New York, 1958.

Travis, Robert J. *The Travis Family. Bowen Press: Decatur, Ga., 1954.*

Webb, Walter P. (ed.). The Handbook of Texas. 2 vols. Texas State Historical Association: Austin, 1952.

Wharton, Clarence R. *The Republic of Texas.* Arthur A. Clarke Co.: Cleveland, 1922.

Williams, Amelia and Eugene C. Barker (eds.). *The Writings of Sam Houston, 1813-1863.* 8 vols. The University of Texas Press: Austin, 1938.

Wortham, Louis J. *A History of Texas From Wilderness to Commonwealth.* Wortham-Molyneaux: Fort Worth, 1924.

Yoakum, Henderson. *History of Texas.* 2 vols. Redfield: New York, 1855.

Articles

Asbury, Samuel C. (ed.). "The Private Journal of Juan Neopnuceno Almonte, February 1-April 16, 1836." *Southwestern Historical Quarterly.* XLVIII (July, 1944): 10-32.

Barker, Eugene C. "Difficulties of a Mexican Revenue Officer In Texas," *Quarterly of the Texas Historical Association.* IV (July, 1900-April, 1901): 194.

_____ "The Organization of the Texas Revolution." *Soutern History Association Publications.* V: 460-461.

_____ "The Texan Revolutionary Army." *Quarterly of the Texas State Historical Association.* IX (April, 1906): 227-261.

Beazley, Julia. "William Barret Travis." *The Texas Review.* IX. (October, 1923): 75-84.

Davis, Robert E. "Travis Draws a Will." *Manuscripts.* (Spring, 1970): 113.

Dobie, J. Frank. "Rose and His Story of the Alamo," in *In The Shadow of History.* Austin, 1939: 9-41.

Frantz, Joe B. "William B. Travis" in *Heroes of Texas.* Waco, 1964: 129-141.

Gallaway, G. Norton. "Sketch of San Antonio." *Magazine of American History.* XV (June, 1886): 532ff.

Greer, James K. (ed.). "The Journal of Ammon Underwood, 1834-1838." *Southwestern Historical Quarterly.* XXII (October, 1928): 136.

Labadie, N. D. "Narrative of Anahuac, or Opening Campaign of the Texas Revolution" in *Texas Almanac for 1859.* Galveston, 1858: 31.

"LaFayette's Visit to Claiborne." *Alabama Historical Quarterly.* 19 (Summer, 1957): 258-278.

Lee, Mrs. A. J. "Some Recollections of Two Texas Pioneer Women." *Texas Methodist Historical Quarterly.* I (January, 1910): 207-213.

Lewis, Carroll. "Fort Anahuac, The Birthplace of the Texas Revolution." *Texana.* VI (Spring, 1968): 1-11.

Looscan, Adele B. "The Old Fort at Anahuac." *Quarterly of the Texas State Historical Association.* II (July, 1889): 21-28.

Lord, Walter. "Myths & Realities of the Alamo" in *The Republic of Texas.* Palo Alto, Calif., 1968: 18-25.

Muir, Andrew Forest (ed.). "The Union Company in Anahuac, 1831-1833." *Southwestern Historical Quarterly.* LXX (October, 1966): 256-271.

Sibley, Marilyn McAdams. "The Burial Place of the Alamo Heroes." *Southwestern Historical Quarterly.* LXX (October, 1966): 272-280.

"General Austin's Order Book for the Campaign of 1835." *Quarterly of the Texas State Historical Association.* XII (July, 1907): 17-47.

"The Reminiscences of Mrs. Dilue Harris." *Quarterly of the Texas State Historical Association.* IV (July 1900-April, 1901): 118ff.

Williams, Amelia. "A Critical Study of the Siege of the Alamo And of the Personnel of Its Defenders." *Southwestern Historical Quarterly.* XXXVI and XXXVII (April, 1933-April, 1934).

Williams, Robert H. "Travis—A Potential Sam Houston." *Southwestern Historical Quarterly.* XL (October, 1936): 154-160.

Zuber, W. P. "The Escape of Rose From The Alamo." *Quarterly of the Texas State Historical Association.* V (July, 1901): 1-11.

Index

207

Beulah Church, 40
Birch, Harvey, 135
Blacksher, Abraham, 41
Boddie, John Bennett, 28
Bonham, James, 29
Bonham, James Butler, 28, 29, 31, 152, 153, 170
Bonham, Milledge L., 29, 30
Borgarra, Anselmo, 176
Bowie, James, 15, 17, 18, 119, 132, 134, 144, 146, 152-158, 162, 163, 165, 172, 177, 178
Bradburn, Col. John Davis, 60, 62, 63, 69-80, 84, 108, 110, 113
Brazoria, Tex., 73, 75, 78, 79, 85, 90, 96, 102, 103, 110, 123
Briscoe, Andrew, 110-112, 134, 135, 177
Burleson, Edward, 133, 136, 138, 139, 143
Burnet, David G., 70, 91, 115
Butler, James, 24
Butler, James A., 93
Bustamente, Anastasio, 68

C

Carbajal, Jose Maria, 71
Cato, William M., 47, 54, 93, 95, 96, 98
Clarke Cty., Ala., 48, 51
Claiborne Academy, 44, 47
Claiborne, Ala., 40-42, 44-50, 52-54, 57, 83
Claiborne *Clarion*, 48
Claiborne *Courier*, 48
Claiborne *Gazette*, 48
Claiborne, Gen. Ferdinand L., 42
Claiborne Herald, 48, 49

Cole, Gabriel, 90
Cloud, Samuel G., 97
Columbia, Tex., 108, 117, 118, 120-122
Conecuh Cty., Ala., 35, 36, 38, 41, 57, 83
Consultation, the, 121, 122, 124, 125, 127, 129-131, 136, 138-141
Cortina, Juan, 77, 80
Cos, Gen. Martin Perfecto de, 109, 113, 114, 118, 120, 121, 124, 127, 128, 131, 133, 135, 146, 151, 158, 160, 175
Cotton, Radford L., 41
Crockett, David, 15, 17, 18, 156-158, 162, 168, 177, 178
Cummings, Rebeca, 94, 95, 97-99, 124, 127, 171

D

Dameron, Christopher, 48
Davis, Jefferson, 26
DeCrow, Mr., 90
De La Pena, Jose Enrique, 175-177
Dellet, James, 9, 43, 45-48, 53, 54, 96, 97
DeLoach, Elizabeth, 27
De Veramendi, Juan Martin, 156
De Veramendi, Maria Ursula, 156
Dimitt, Capt. Philip, 146
Dickinson, Angelina, 175
Dickinson, Capt. Almeron, 173
Dickinson, Mrs. Susannah, 173, 175, 178
Dinsmore, Silas, 84
Dooley, John, 22
Dow, Lorenzo, 25

Draughan, James, 43
Duque, Col. Don Francisco, 175

E

Eastin, Thomas, 48
Edgefield District (Cty.), S.C.,
22, 24, 25, 27, 30, 33, 55, 57
Edwards, Monroe, 76, 77, 96
Euphemien Lodge, No. 13, 41
Evergreen Academy, 40

F

Fannin, Col. James, 132-136,
138, 140, 141, 144, 154, 162,
169, 170, 174
Federal Road, the, 34
Fisher, Goerge, 63, 69, 72-74,
110
Forsythe, Capt., 148
Fort Bend, Cty., Tex., 92
Fort Claiborne, 36, 38, 43
Fort Loudon, 23
Fort Prince George, 23
Fort Sepulga, 35
Fort Settlement, 129
Fort Stoddard, 34
Fort Teran, 69
Fountain, Raymond, 54
Frantz, Joe B., 17
Fredonia Rebellion, the, 67
Freeman, Benjamin, 111
French, L. C., 48

G

Galveston, Tex., 68, 69, 72, 73,
97, 110, 111
Galveston Bay and Texas Land
Co., 70
Glen, James, 23, 24
Goliad, Tex., 69, 144, 145, 162,
164, 169
Gonzales, Tex., 102, 111, 128,
129, 148, 162, 164, 165, 169,
170, 174
Gosport, Ala., 48, 54, 57
Grant, Dr. James, 144, 145, 152,
154
Grayson, Peter, 103
Gritten, Edward, 121
Gutierrez de Lara, Bernardo, 65

H

Hanks, Wyatt, 138, 142
Hannah, 77
Hardin, William, 111
Harrisburg, Tex., 111, 113, 115,
116, 118
Harris, David, 90, 93, 111, 115
Harris, DeWitt Clinton, 15, 112,
113
Harris, Mrs. Dilue, 91
Harris, Robert, 108, 113
Hart, Reuben, 36
Haskins, Francis J., 92
Henderson, William, 44
Henry, Miss, 94
Herrera, Blaz, 159
Herrera, Gen. Simon, 65

209

211

212

Weems, Mason Locke, 25
Wharton, William H., 100, 101, 119, 129, 140
White, James Taylor, 61
Wigfall, Louis T., 28
Wightman, Mr., 90
Wilkins, Mrs. Jane, 85
Wilkinson, Gen. James, 65
Williams, Amelia, 16, 17, 28
Williams, Samuel, 109, 113
Williams, S. B., 59
Williamson, Robert M. ("Three-Legged Willie"), 59, 60, 76, 84, 85, 87, 91, 93, 102-104, 106

Wilson, Robert, 90, 93, 111
Winfrey, Dorman, 17
Wolf, James, 25
Woodruff, Mr., 92

Z

Zavala, Lorenzo de, 70, 119, 121
Zuber, W. P., 172, 173

Afterword: Travis

One Chief Rol'd Among the Rest

Rarely does a historian get a second chance to express his views on a subject once it reaches print. Then, for all time, for ill or good, he is on record. This will be the case so long as the world continues to use the printed page. Perhaps in a little while we will have no printed books, only floppy disks. Then we can keep our work in a constant state of revision and everyone can tune in via a modem to our data base and find out our latest thoughts and findings. In the idiom of my native East Texas, you can lick your calf over again and again.

Probably my day will have passed before this comes to pass. For me, it is enough that Eakin Press asked me to revisit my friend William Barret Travis twenty years after the initial appearance of my biography of him.

Some things have changed since last I visited Travis, and, of course, some have remained the same. For example, in the way of the dead, he is still five months shy of his twenty-seventh birthday, while I, in the way of the living, have aged twenty years. In that time I have witnessed the election of several presidents of radically diverse political philosophies, seen my country held hostage in Iran and Lebanon, and learned of a new danger to society in the form of Acquired Immune Deficiency Syndrome. John Wayne and Elvis Presley have passed from the scene. In other words, I have aged: Travis has not.

But do I still see him as I did then, in my less mature if far from callow years? The answer is, for the most part, I do. I must admit that since *Travis* appeared in 1976, other duties and other interests have kept me from earnestly continuing the search for the real Travis. I had said my piece and was, and I remain, reasonably content with the result. Most historians, lay and professional, agreed with my conclusions; a few did not. For example, a review in the *Austin American–Statesman* said: "McDonald's book is being billed as the first complete scholarly biography of Travis, but readers shouldn't let that scare them off. The text only occasionally sinks into tedium [presumably a synonym for 'scholarly'] — the author puzzles, for example, for a full page over Travis' disputed birth date — and for most of the book's pages it is a lively and enlightening narrative of Texas' most obscure hero."

The review I liked best, which appeared in the *Corpus Christi Caller,* began: "A book entitled *Travis* caught my eye the other day because my grandmother was a Travis. Not that I am a descendant of the Alamo commander for he had but one son and he left no children, but with this *Roots* business, I picked up the book out of curiosity to see if there was any relationship. I'm glad I did. The author makes a man of flesh out of a statue. William Barret Travis appears in Texas history as a hot-headed, pompous dandy who arrived at the Alamo in time to argue with James Bowie, then die in a flame of glory." The review continues for a few column inches with a synopsis of the book, including some of the less attractive aspects of Travis' life, and concludes by saying that it is little wonder that William Travis was not much mentioned in their discussions of family history.

Most reviews by newspapers were complimentary, and even the academic journals had kind things to say. Academicians always have to be cute in their reviews, so, while William Vaughn of North Texas State University, writing for the *Journal of Southern History,* found that *Travis* ". . . is generally written in an appealing and concise manner, it is not until the last chapter that Travis emerges as a vibrant human being." He then excused me for not having much to work with, but lamented that there were too few illustrations.

And Lonn Taylor, writing for the *Southwestern Historical*

Quarterly, said, "On the whole, this is a competent book, but there is nothing new in it, and one suspects that there will never be anything new about Travis until some new cache of documents comes to light. When they do, this reviewer hopes that Professor McDonald finds them, because he is a lively writer who deserves the chance to do justice to his subject."

To tell the truth, I really haven't looked for that new cache of documents, but I have taken consolation from an observation by Cervantes that I have found to be profound: "He that publishes a book runs a very great hazard." I thought then — and still do — that I knew as much about Travis as Taylor or Vaughn. Besides, I long ago stopped writing for professional historians. Except perhaps in a few narrow post holes of my study, all of them already know what I know and many of them can express it better. So, for the greater part of my career I have written for, and mostly spoken to, the general public, the men and women who read a book or an article because they want to learn something from it, who will attend a Civil War Round Table or a local history society meeting because they love history and fellowship with their kind. To popularize history is to bastardize it in the eyes of some of my purer colleagues of the academy, and I concede: in some respects they are correct. But not in all. I have never understood why history must be dull to be "good" or, in the word of the *American–Statesman* reviewer, "tedious" to be scholarly. I aim for both and probably miss both marks, but that is my path.

So, after twenty years, let us again look at my friend Travis, a man of many rivers. We will build on the pioneer work of Samuel Asbury of Texas A&M College, who began the twentieth-century search for Travis in the 1920s. Asbury was the first historian to visit the Travis family in Alabama or their former residence in South Carolina. He was mostly a collector of data and documents, so he did not produce a biography, but before his labor ended meaningful writing on Travis appeared in academic thesis form by Amelia Williams and Ruby Mixon. Williams' "A Critical Study of the Siege of the Alamo and of the Personality of Its Defenders" set the style for all subsequent writing on the Alamo, as did Mixon's "William Barret Travis: His Life and Letters" for Travis himself. The latter's greatest contribution is the collection, in one place, of most of the extant Travis materials. Upon the base established by these two women historians rests the better known work of Lon Tinkle in *Thirteen Days of Glory,* Walter Lord's *A Time to Stand,* John Myers' *The Alamo,* Joe B. Frantz' biographical essay in *Heroes of Texas,* Virgil Baugh's *Rendezvous at the Alamo,* the juvenile biography of *Travis* by Walter McCalef, Martha Ann Turner's biography, and, for that matter, my own work. It is impossible to overemphasize the debt owed by so many Texas historians to Williams and Mixon. If my work contains any original contribution it is probably in the chapters dealing with the interpretation of Travis' motives at the Alamo and with his birth and early life in South Carolina and his formative years in Alabama. At the time I visited both places on research trips I was the first to have done so since Asbury.

One might wonder why so important a figure as Travis has attracted so few writers. One reason is that for forty years everyone expected Mixon to publish her thesis, which she never did. Another reason is that unlike Houston, Crockett, or Austin, men important before the Texas Revolution, Travis was an obscurity before the war, was negatively regarded for much of its course, and died before its end. He also was much younger, nearly twenty years younger, than the prominent leaders, and his motives for migration to Texas and participation in its revolution — especially the decisions at the Alamo — are guarded by his death before the revolutionary war ended.

But the principal reason for so little being written about Travis is the paucity of sources. For most of his life prior to coming to Texas he remains an anonymous figure of the American frontier. Often he deliberately covered his tracks, as when he told officials in 1831 that he was a widower, so one must wonder more at what remains than what does not. And even more importantly, there are at least three Travises: a South Carolina Travis, a red-headed kid who played at the Bonham house and eventually turned up in Texas and became a hero; an Alabama Travis, more remembered than revered, who beat the odds to earn glory in the West; and, of course, a Texas Travis, a complicated thing unto itself, twice a cause of trouble in Anahuac, despite his youth a man of importance in the

Texas War Party, and, because of the manner of his death, forever fixed in the pantheon of Texas heroes.

I suppose I have read as much about Travis as most Texas historians, and frankly I am weary of such adjectives as "heroic," "gallant," and "defiant." It is not that Travis lacked these qualities. He clearly possessed them, as did many of his contemporaries. It is just that I have seen him in more human ways. Love him or hate him, think of him as sinner or saint, legend or less, I proposed that we call him simply a man, a Travis, "as one chief rol'd among the rest," and accept him for that.

The search for this Travis, this flesh and blood and very alive human being, requires some "givens." For one, we might as well admit that Travis was one of the most headstrong, opportunistic fellows imaginable. Remember that the *second* most quoted Travis letter from the Alamo, to David Ayers, who had custody of his son, speaks of "making a splendid fortune." The Travis most of us meet is the white-washed character presented in seventh-grade Texas history courses or viewed in the seventh-grade-level advertisements and memorials that appear yearly around Alamo day. This image features a tall man, about forty years of age, who is handsomely dressed in waistcoat and tails, Wellington boots, and a defiant look. In his hand he holds a sabre and his gritted countenance challenges the Mexicans to assault the walls of the Alamo in perpetuity.

As I observed twenty years ago, this movie star image, this legend we have grown up with, was born of the countless references to Travis' gallantry, bravery, and loyalty that abound in the biographical sketches and advertisements. Most of the sketches are divided into two parts. The first deals with his first twenty-two years, the time that was really the making of him on the American frontier. Usually this requires a few paragraphs at most. They usually conclude with rhetorical questions about why he left an established business and marriage and migrated to Texas in 1831. The second part of the sketch picks up the Travis story at the first Anahuac disturbance, traces his rise in the politics of the Texas Revolution, and ends in glory at the Alamo. This Travis emerges as a historical curiosity. Everyone has heard of him but few know much about him. He resembles a tropical hurricane that rises in the east from a shadowy source, passes its building time in obscurity until its velocity cannot be ignored, then quickly departs, leaving a vivid memory of a brief moment of center-stage activity.

The search for a more real Travis must be more complete than this. This Travis, this man of many rivers, this "chief rol'd among the rest," traced his line to a Travers who crossed the Channel in the eleventh century to help William conquer England. Travers' self-composed epitaph in the Freery at Preston recalls a bold man:

> *I Travers by birth a Norman*
> *To gain victorious conquest*
> *With William Conqueror in I came*
> *As one Chief rol'd among the rest . . .*

The earliest Travers to cross the Atlantic to Virginia, Edward, came in 1626. For two centuries the Traverses, like everyone else in the developing American frontier, struggled to survive. In time their name became Travis, and another traditional family name, Berwick, elided into Barrot, and finally became Barret.

The line included a Barrot Travis, who begot a Mark Travis and an Alexander Travis. Mark begot William Barret Travis, with the assistance of Jemima Stallworth, in Edgefield District, now Saluda County, South Carolina, on August 9, 1809. There is a persistent rumor that he was illegitimate. This sprang from the fact that Mark Travis did have an illegitimate son, Taliaferro Travis, who was accepted into his stepmother's home completely. Part of the tale suggests that Travis' middle name, Barret, came from his alleged method of arrival as an abandoned child suspended from the top bar, or rail, of his father's corral fence. If anyone did so it would have been Taliaferro, not William, but even Taliaferro did not arrive that way.

Travis' Uncle Alexander, an itinerant and forceful Baptist preacher, became something of a family patriarch. When the Travis fortunes suffered significantly in the financial crisis that culminated in the Panic of 1819, Alexander Travis searched for greener pastures in the West. He found them in Conecuh

County, Alabama, where he helped establish the towns of Sparta and Evergreen. William Travis crossed his first of many rivers to reach his new home in 1818. Far from being the scion of aristocrats, as he is often presented, especially in film, Travis' father was a dirt-farmer and his uncle often walked to preaching assignments barefoot to save shoe leather.

They earned their living from the soil, but Travis' precociousness saved him from a permanent sentence as a farmer. He attended the Evergreen Academy, then moved a few miles west to attend a school taught by a Professor McCurdy in Monroe County in a community later called Monroeville. Travis learned his letters and figures sufficiently to be able to help with the tutoring of the younger or less advanced, and met a girl named Rosanna Cato. They were married on October 26, 1828, and nine months and two weeks later became the parents of Charles Edward. In an era before chemical or intercessory birth control devices this was not unusual, but it also led to speculation that the couple had been intimate prior to their marriage. In a time when "living in" replaces marriage for many, even this should not shock us, but we do not want our heroes to be *too* human, so the debunkers have delighted in, and the worshipers have ignored, this suggestion of premarital impropriety. It has also led to speculation that suspected infidelity on Rosanna's part was the primary motivation for Travis' immigration to Texas in 1831. This latter assumption is possibly true, but that is getting ahead of the story.

From 1828 until his departure from Alabama three years later, Travis gave every impression of becoming an established young man in his community. One might even liken him to a budding Jaycee. He read for the law in the offices of Judge James Dellet in Claiborne, Alabama, and eventually became his tutor's partner; he established a newspaper in Claiborne; he joined the Masonic Lodge, evidently by dispensation because he was not yet twenty-one years of age when he received his Entered Apprentice Degree; and he became an adjutant in the Alabama militia.

Then, without any recorded explanation, he mounted his big black horse one day in the late spring of 1831, crossed the Alabama River, and headed for Texas. He abandoned his practice, his business, his wife and son, and most importantly, his unborn daughter, Susan Isabella.

We do not lack for suggestions of causes for his actions; what we lack is evidence. One story suggests that he defended a man accused of murder and could only get the man off by confessing to the act himself — allegedly under the protection of a Masonic oath of secrecy to Judge Dellet — and fled to Texas with the judge's approval. Another suggests that he left after someone cut off the tail of his horse. Probably Travis did kill someone, an Alabama River gambler whom he suspected of fathering the infant in Rosanna's womb, and left for Texas without facing trial, not so much from fear of the verdict as from embarrassment that he had not protected his home. I emphasize that no one knows for sure why he left, only that he crossed the river and never returned. When he arrived in Texas in May he first told authorities that he was a widower. He made no move to divorce Rosanna, but he did agree to one when she asked for it five years later.

But Travis was not lonely in Texas, and the move in 1831 brought him new opportunities in law, in land, and with the ladies in Texas. Fortunately for historians, Travis kept a kind of memoranda-journal during a part of his life in Texas, and this and his surviving correspondence are about all that remain to instill life into his memory. He came to Texas via New Orleans and settled in the Anahuac community. Anahuac is on flat ground and only a short distance from the open waters of the Gulf. A port of entry with a vigorous trade, it was a good place for a young lawyer to locate. Texas seemed blessed, some would say cursed, with many men who thought of themselves as lawyers, or who at least lived off the periphery of the law as land transfer agents, title searchers, business go-betweens, and manipulators. Travis did all of these things, but he also did trial work, handling cases ranging from cattle stealing to more serious, even capital, crimes. Most of his cases, however, involved property disputes.

Travis' practice carried him over the country and within a few years he was well known and he himself knew many powerful Texans. More and more he became associated with the explosive element in Texas politics. When a War Party became sufficiently established for recognition, he was one of its leaders. Politics is the natural playground of legalists, and Travis enjoyed it as much as the next. His politics, however, hardly seemed like enjoyment. It was more often than not quite serious, even deadly, and led to his arrest on one occasion and to his being posted an outlaw on another.

The first of these events, which illustrates Travis the lawyer as well as the politician (and incidentally as an opportunist who utilized the situation for political and potentially financial gain), occurred in Anahuac shortly after his arrival. The Mexican government had established a customs collection officer in the town in the summer of 1830, and had assigned John Davis Bradburn, late of Kentucky and now in the Mexican service, to command a small garrison. Bradburn was a poor choice. He was soon at odds with the community because of decisions regarding sailing permits. Protests only made the situation more delicate. Finally, following an alleged rape of a woman in Anahuac by one of Bradburn's Mexican soldiers, Travis and several others administered a tar-and-feather and rail-riding party for the amorous soldier. Bradburn responded by the arrest of the participants, and one of the sparks of the Texas revolution was struck. Travis himself was arrested for pulling a prank on Bradburn that unnerved the army commander. The jailing and subsequent freeing of Travis and the other Anahuac prisoners made them all important men among the resisters of the Mexican authority, and it particularly marked him as a man whom trouble followed. Even the moderate, not to say conservative, among the Texans began to look at him with anxiety.

As the revolution matured, Travis would again and again be among those who advocated haste in the independence movement. Once he even led a group back to Anahuac after he moved to San Felipe to depose the Mexican authority there. This last act caused his temporary eclipse in Texas politics because it was too rash, too quick, too bold for the times. But his rise to the secretaryship of the *ayuntamiento* of San Felipe obviously was made possible by his first involvement, and his subsequent place in the movement for independence was linked to the latter. It was not that each move was calculated or contrived, but he did seem to sense when the time was right to impose himself in a situation so as to be prominent in it, and to capitalize on the prominence. So it would be at the Alamo itself.

But before discussing that, we need to consider the humanity of Travis. It is here that Travis' journal or diary is of greatest help, for it is our closest look into his mind. It obviously was not kept with the idea that anyone would ever see it, although he was discrete enough to couch its most personal passages in Spanish. Still, most Anglos and certainly nearly all Mexicans in Texas could have fathomed this, so it is possible that he just liked to speak of love in a more romantic language. Whatever his motive, the diary makes it plain that Travis did not lead a monk's life in Texas.

Women were not Travis' only indulgence. His diary indicates that he frequently gambled at faro and other games of chance, and he dutifully recorded the sums he won or lost. Travis also took a drink now and again, and he would pull a prank on a friend or a foe. He was, in short, a rather normal young man who lived his life as normal young men did on the frontier Texas of the 1830s. He was, after all, only twenty-six years and seven months old when he died at the Alamo.

And there is no reason to assume that his humanity was limited to the more venal pursuits. Travis was also a compassionate man when meeting persons in need, tenderhearted even, and possessed of a strong sense of justice. He was a promoter of organized religion, on one occasion writing to the Methodist Missionary Board to request a mission in Texas. He often took small gifts to the children of friends, and his visits were memorable events for them. He was a solicitous father to his own son after he came to Texas, and, as we have seen, some of his last thoughts were of Charles.

In sum Travis was a complex personality, the sort to which people of all kinds warmed, especially if they liked the rough-and-ready style of man.

When the resistance to Mexico started in earnest, Travis was committed to Governor Henry Smith. Within a few weeks he rose from lieutenant to lieutenant colonel in the Texas army. This set him apart from the majority of Texas fighting men, most of whom served only in volunteer capacities and when they wanted to. He served commendably as a scout in the early action before the taking of Bexar in December 1835, chafed at in the recruiting duty to which he was assigned, and questioned the orders which took him back to San Antonio in January 1836. Intended for a subordinate's role, Travis on the departure of James C. Neill became the ranking officer. Travis accepted the command of the Alamo and with it the consequence of staying within the walls while the siege formed around him.

Generations have wondered why he did not leave when escape was so easy, at least at first, when he even had orders which would have permitted a discretionary leave taking. The answer must be that he felt there was something to gain. The temper of his letters, at least until March 3, reveals a confidence that victory was possible, even probable, if support would come. If it had, what would have been gained? Since most of the Alamo garrison save the Gonzales reinforcement of approximately thirty men were recent immigrants, the simple answer is land. But the Alamo would not have been necessary for that. There must have been a grander motivation. It seems that Crockett was seeking a military reputation to become a serious presidential candidate in 1836 or 1840 in the United States; perhaps Travis had equal, if not political, ambitions in Texas. There is no evidence that he coveted political office, but the possibility of money, land, prestige, and even empire following an Alamo victory is intriguing. What else could have kept him there? Nothing had kept him in Alabama.

There was redemption in the blood of the Alamo, and no matter why he stayed he is now enshrined in the minds of Texans who remember the deed. No other loss in history is so appreciated as the Alamo. But it is hard to believe that Travis would have been there, or stayed, if this were his only anticipated reward. He was too much of a hell-for-leather man to settle for that. And it does not demean him to suggest that he had practical motives or to suggest that he saw opportunities in the revolution. To see him as a practical man is to see him as a man, like us, who lived life, not just history.

Travis died early in the assault, a single bullet piercing his head. Later, after his body was identified by five separate witnesses to verify his death, Travis' remains perished in the pyres

Santa Anna used to dispose of his foes. Soon Travis and his men were celebrated — and mourned — throughout Texas and the United States. He and his men transcended defeat and became legends. Far from a forgotten *beau geste,* their dying gave them immortality.

As I wrote twenty years ago: "It is easy to lose Travis when the story of the revolution grows larger, to forget the individual in the cumulative accomplishment. But ironically it is easier to remember this last part of the life and to forget its seasoning in South Carolina, in Alabama, Anahuac, and San Felipe, his crossings of the Alabama, the Mississippi, the Sabine, the Trinity, the Brazos — finally the San Antonio. But his life was the sum of his crossings. His life in those first years was the making of him, for he remained to the end what he had become through youth and growing maturity in a frontier setting — an American, a Southerner, a Texan, a man, a Travis, like his ancestor, a 'chief rol'd among the rest.' He had crossed many rivers to become a chief. As permanent as time, the Alabama, the Mississippi, the Sabine, even the San Antonio, rolled on. His crossings were meaningful to him, left their watermarks on his life, but all were behind him that cold morning on March 6 when he raced up a cannon embankment to meet his fate in the form of a Mexican's bullet. If there was one more river to cross that morning, it was wide and deep."

Note: Much of this material appeared in the Kathryn Stoner O'Connor Lectures on Texas History at Victoria College and is the first essay in the series. It is reproduced here, with modifications, by permission. What has not been modified is my basic understanding of Travis, "One Chief Rol'd Among the Rest."